Praise for *The Secret Language of Business*

"If you want to communicate more powerfully, influence with greater impact, and lead more effectively, you will want to read this book. Packed with research and real-world application, *The Secret Language of Business* will help you in far more than business. Use it, and the information in this book can change your life."

—Kevin Eikenberry, author of *Remarkable Leadership: Unleashing Your Leadership Potential One Skill at a Time*

"A revealing tour through the fine points of the 'nonconscious' mind, and how little details make *all* the difference! This book is an authoritative shortcut to using powerful nonverbal communication skills to read others, and, to send intentional and deeply effective messages to get the results you want."

—David Garfinkel, author of *Advertising Headlines That Make You Rich*

"Ninety-three percent of your effectiveness is determined by your nonverbal cues. Kevin Hogan divulges what you're unconsciously communicating and decodes what others are revealing about themselves. Read this book before you ask for a raise. Hide this book from your vendors. *The Secret Language of Business* will give you an unfair business advantage as clients' inner thoughts become transparent."

—Ben Mack, best-selling author of *Think Two Products Ahead* and former Senior Vice President, BBDO

"This is a book that is needed by everyone who communicates (okay, that is *everyone*!). Kevin Hogan manages to give a comprehensive overview of nonverbal communication while giving depth, advanced skills, and surprising facts. I can't wait to share the ideas I learned with my coaching clients!"

—Larina Kase, PsyD, MBA, business psychologist and coauthor of the *New York Times* best-selling book *The Confident Speaker*

THE SECRET LANGUAGE OF BUSINESS

THE SECRET LANGUAGE OF BUSINESS

How to Read Anyone in 3 Seconds or Less

KEVIN HOGAN

WILEY

John Wiley & Sons, Inc.

Published by John Wiley & Sons, Inc., Hoboken, New Jersey.
Published simultaneously in Canada.

For general information on our other products and services or for technical support, please contact our Customer Care Department within the United States at (800) 762-2974, outside the United States at (317) 572-3993 or fax (317) 572-4002.

Wiley also publishes its books in a variety of electronic formats. Some content that appears in print may not be available in electronic books. For more information about Wiley products, visit our web site at www.wiley.com.

Library of Congress Cataloging-in-Publication Data:
Hogan, Kevin.
   The secret language of business : how to read anyone in 3 seconds or less / Kevin Hogan.
     p. cm.
   Includes bibliographical references.
   ISBN 978-0-470-22289-8 (cloth)
   1. Body language.   2. Nonverbal communication in the workplace.   I. Title.
BF637.N66H64 2008
153.6′9—dc22

                                                        2007025169

Printed in the United States of America.

10 9 8 7 6 5 4 3 2 1

For
Mark, Jessica, and Katie

Contents

Acknowledgments

T hanks to Matt Holt, "my" editor, and John Wiley & Sons, Inc. The staff at Cape Cod Compositors, too. Thanks also go to the people in my life who make it better. Michelle Drum Matteson, Lisa McLellan, Jennifer Battaglino, Ken Owens, Mark Ryan, Bob Beverley, Blair Warren, Scott and Carmen Schluter, Devin and Rachel Hastings.

Thanks to my *Inner Circle* for making me better at what I do. Bryan Lenihan, Paul Thomas, Gary May, JJ Austrian, Sonya Lenzo, Steve Chambers, Craig Ernst, John Bedosky, Eliot Hoppe, April Braswell, Jimmy Slagle, Gail Hurt, Phil Hamilton, Duane Cunningham, Erwin van den Boogaard, Michael Neumann, Luis Lopez, Phil Graves, Sami Miettinen, and Aleta Batz.

Introduction

Welcome to *The Secret Language of Business: How to Read Anyone in 3 Seconds or Less*, a book that will have a powerful impact on your life. The information presented here is based on a combination of academic research, science, practical application, and over 20 years of experience in the teaching, communication, and influence professions.

If you're ready to embark on a journey of learning, self-discovery, and the kind of real-world practical information you've always wanted but could never find, then you're in the right place.

Regular updates to this book will be posted at www.kevinhogan. com. There is a secret link at the bottom of the page. It says "Language." Click there and join other readers for free updates . . . forever.

The Purpose of This Book

There are hundreds of books available on the subject of body language and nonverbal communication.

They range from the purely academic to the purely incidental and everywhere in between. Throughout my years of teaching and professional speaking, one of the most consistent complaints I have heard from students and professionals is their inability to find a book that is reputable, engaging, and applicable to the real world in which they work and live.

In other words, if you're like them, you want to know what other people are thinking. You want to know what messages others are sending.

You want to know if they like you.

You want to know if they are deceiving you.

You want to be able to read what kind of people they are from looking at them and the things around them.

And, maybe most importantly, you want to make the right and best impression you can on others, especially the first time you meet them.

There is a widespread hunger for accurate information on this subject, but few, if any, resources combine the facts with useful practical applications.

And that's why I wrote this book.

This book is designed to help you wade through the external noise and confusion of other resources and focus on the information that is most relevant to your needs. It is not strictly academic, nor is it strictly self-help. It is a combination of these two things that will take you through all of the most important aspects of nonverbal communication and how it influences every part of your daily life.

I've devoured a lot of nonverbal communication material over the last two decades.

As far as this book is concerned, it's hard to know when to say "when."

A lot of people want to know what every gesture and movement means.

As you will find out, even the person performing the gesture or behaving in a certain way typically doesn't know what the gesture means.

Getting past how the brain works (which we will only touch on here) and how it directs most of nonverbal communication, we'll talk about the core factors of the Secret Language of Business.

The context in which X occurred.

The culture in which X occurred.

The person's catalog of reactions and responses.

There are hundreds, if not thousands, of contexts within which nonverbal communication occurs. (Being at the grocery store vs. watching TV at home.)

There are literally dozens of cultures per country on the globe, making for easily thousands of cultures and significant differences between cultures. (Society family vs. Gangsta Rap dudes.)

There are literally hundreds of gestures, signals, movements.

That combines for trillions of possible meanings that culture, context, and reaction can ultimately have.

That's a whole bunch of possibilities.

That was the biggest challenge about writing this book: writing an eminently useful book without turning it into a concordance of situations.

What to Expect from This Book

Expect to be a little nervous.

The study of nonverbal communication including body language is often a study of stereotypes and prejudging.

Those words make my heart skip a beat.

A lot of people don't want to hear that. (Like you and me.)

But it's an enormous part of the comprehension equation.

You have to think both stereotype and prejudice on a few different levels to master reading other people's nonverbal behavior.

Stereotypes are just that. They are generalizations about people based upon certain characteristics they possess.

Research is abundantly clear that women stereotype more accurately than men do. Women "get people" better than men do. It's not a close contest. (Except when it comes to deception where men perform as well as women do and stereotype the deceptive behaviors of others as well as women do.)

Prejudice is prejudging people.

That's what reading people is all about.

Breathe...

Neither of these actions is encouraged in society because they can lead people to behave unkindly toward others.

There's nothing "nice" or "mean" about reading body language and nonverbal communication. It's not good or bad, it's simply reading and interpreting.

It's a very real-life experience.

For better or worse, you must be effective at making generalizations and prejudging.

That said, I'm not encouraging prejudice from a *behavioral* standpoint.

In other words, just because someone is black or white, male or female doesn't mean you shouldn't hire them or date them.

It means there are characteristics that are often correlated with others of the same skin color, gender, religion, school affiliation, and so forth, typically *within a given culture.*

In other words, you probably won't find gangsta rap popular in Nigeria, Haiti, or in the Australian outback. It's not the skin color, it's how people are drawn to each other in a culture by their similarities and then how they bond as a community.

Culture is huge in understanding nonverbal communication.

Within a culture, sometimes those correlations are cause/effect. Sometimes they are causation.

There is a big difference between causation and correlation, but this book is not about that difference.

This book is about reading people and being good at it.

This book is about sending nonverbal messages that are likely to influence others.

This book is a frank and intelligent discussion about complex and politically incorrect stuff. (And sometimes I lighten things up a bit . . .)

At no point in this book do I intentionally offend anyone. At no point do I intentionally attempt to stir a pot of controversy.

What you will discover here is factual information collected by the smartest minds on the planet as far as nonverbal communication, anthropology, social psychology, and neuroscience go.

Then I take all of that and hopefully make it easy to read and not all that painful.

I have prejudices. Lots of them. Conscious mind and nonconscious mind.

It's important to recognize them in yourself and not ignore them.

If you say, "I'm not prejudiced," you are practicing the art of self deception. You are prejudiced by nature of being a human being.

Recognize it, and master the emotions that go along with it.

Be good to people.

Six years ago, I got to moderate a really neat event: Speed Dating.

There were 16 men and 16 women who would rotate throughout the evening, spending four, count'em four, minutes with each other.

At the end of the four minutes they would tick off on an index card whether they wanted to date the person.

I ultimately guided three of these events. Two in Minneapolis and one in Seattle.

What I learned was fascinating.

1. Women wanted to date far fewer men than the number of women men were willing to date. (We're so much more flexible and accommodating . . . or desperate.)

2. Ninety-three percent of women told me that they knew in the first 30 seconds whether they would be willing to date the person again.

3. Almost as many men said they knew "right away," "instantly," "within three seconds."

4. The more people someone wanted to date, the fewer people wanted to date (usually) him.

The lessons of those three evenings are many and could fill a book themselves.

But for now, realize that I thought these people were prejudging each of their dates that night.

And then I realized I may not have been correct.

Perhaps we know our yardstick very well and do know in three seconds.

The Secret Language of Business is nonverbal communication, but nonverbal communication is not simply body language. You'll find out more shortly.

You will read about the very basics of body language and the power it has to influence attitudes, actions, and outcomes. You will learn about the key elements of body language and how they influence communication, as well as the effects of the things people wear, the symbols they surround themselves with, the context, environment, proxemics, personal status, income, physical features, and chronemics.

And don't worry . . . I'll make it easy to understand.

Where I say, "There's a lot of research," please accept that as a fact. Otherwise we have to go get 60 journal articles and footnote each idea. Let's keep this simple but very accurate.

With this solid examination of technical aspects under your belt, you will move on to the chapters that I believe are the heart and soul of this book.

They focus on the real-world impact of body language and nonverbal communication on personal interactions of all kinds. From the business world to the personal world, you'll discover important information and insights that you can put to good use right away . . . even with your kids.

What's going to amaze you is that what takes place in the office is very similar to what takes place in sexual relationships and among family members.

The final chapters look at self-examination and how you can take a look at your own nonverbal communication. They also discuss how you can make the most of the power of The Secret Language of Business in your everyday life.

For most people, everyday life includes working with a diverse array of people from other countries and other cultures, whether it's face to face in the workplace or using modern technology to interact across the globe. This is an increasingly important area given our increasingly globalized world, so I have included a chapter on body language and other cultures as well.

"Kevin, when you come to Italy to give your presentation to the private investment bankers, don't wear black like you did last time."

"Why not, Ronald?"

"Because it is boring."

"What should I wear?"

"Anything but black."

Great. And he was serious.

A lot of Europeans take color pretty seriously.

I wore bright blue and felt like a lighthouse.

Throughout the book, you will find well-researched, accurate information that reflects the most current knowledge on the topic of body language and nonverbal communication. Everything you read in this book is based on fact and research, not on someone's guesswork or untested ideas.

My own experiences and observations are also included along the way in an effort to bring you an engaging combination of academic and real–world content. But my observations are only that. And, when something is my observation, I'll let you know.

How to Use This Book

Just as no two people are exactly alike, there is no single best way to use this book. It contains a wide array of information and applications that may or may not apply to your specific circumstances and needs. That's okay, though, because even if a particular subject area is not directly applicable to your life right now, chances are it will be at some point. What you learn now will carry with you over time, and you might just be surprised at how and when you are able to apply it.

In general, this is how I recommend you use this book:

1. Read each chapter thoroughly. Make note of anything that particularly stands out for you, whether it reflects your own experience or you simply find it interesting.

2. Pay attention to the takeaway pages at the end of each chapter. These pages capture the key points that are important for you to grasp from that chapter. If you find something in the takeaways that seems unfamiliar or doesn't make sense to you, review the chapter again to get a better understanding of that particular point.

3. Use the worksheet pages at the end of each chapter. These pages will have questions, activities, or exercises of various sorts to help reinforce the content of that chapter. It may be tempting to pass over the worksheet and move on to the next chapter, but I strongly encourage you not to do that. Take the time to stop and do the worksheet before moving on because it will help you truly learn and apply the information in ways that are more impacting and long lasting.

4. Share what you learn with other people. Talk about what you learn with someone else, such as a friend, relative, peer, or colleague. Ask for their thoughts and perspectives on the various topics and get them to share their own experiences in the real world. It's a great way to spend a coffee break or lunch hour, and you will both take away new knowledge.

5. Read it with a friend. Partner with another person to read the book and do the activities along the way. (Like a two-person book club.) I have found that the most effective way to do this is for each person to have a copy of the book, and then work through the book one chapter at a time. Read through the chapter and take notes on your own, then get together to discuss the chapter and what you learned. You can do the worksheet together if you like or each do it on your own and then compare results.

6. Have fun! The study of The Secret Language of Business and the application of its principles can be a whole lot of fun if you let it be. Look at people on TV to see examples of some of the topics in this book—it's an eye-opening experience, to say the least. Have a telephone conversation in front of the mirror so you can watch your own body language. If you're especially brave, find a friend who is willing to be videotaped having a conversation with you and then let the camera roll while you have a cup of coffee or tea together. Then go back and watch the video together and see what you notice.

A lot of the stuff in this book can get heavy. So I try and get out of my academic tone and into my natural rhythm often.

In the end, how you choose to use this book is entirely up to you. I encourage you to consider some of my suggestions for its use, but the most important thing is for you to use it in a way that creates the maximum benefit and learning for you. That is my primary goal: to help you take the information I've gathered and use it to improve all aspects of your life. Use it to give you an edge in life. Use it to master communication at all levels.

Regardless of how you decide to use it, I'd love to hear from you when you're done. Let me know what worked for you, what didn't work for you, and what you might like to learn more about. This helps us all to improve, and who knows—you might see something you suggested in a future update of the book!

Best regards,

Kevin Hogan, Psy.D.

About the Author

Dr. Kevin Hogan is widely agreed to be one of the nation's leading body language experts. He has over 20 years of experience in the academic study of body language as well as the practical, real-world application of body language and nonverbal communication. His consulting services are in significant demand. Kevin has worked with government, companies, and organizations as diverse as Fortis MeesPierson, Boeing, Precorp, Microsoft, 3M, Aunt Anne's, Cargill, Great Clips, the United States Postal Service, and Starbucks to name a few.

He also frequently serves as an expert resource for news and print media sources such as CNN, Fox News, CBS, the New York Times, the BBC, Redbook, Playboy, Selling Power, Sales and Marketing Management, Maxim, Cosmopolitan, and others.

For more information, please visit www.kevinhogan.com.

1

The Secret Language of Business

C ool title.
Best part is that it's a pretty perfect description of nonverbal communication.

You might notice that I use the phrases "nonverbal communication" and "body language" almost interchangeably in this book at times. So let's define each of these right away.

The fact is that body language is a subdomain of nonverbal communication.

Body language refers to body position, gestures, eye contact, and . . . the body!

Nonverbal communication includes those things but also includes how people dress, societal norms on dress and behavior, the jewelry people wear, the tattoos people reveal, the distance people stand from each other, the way people use time, the way people use space . . . even the tone and pitch of people's voices.

And it is at this level of nonverbal communication that The Secret Language of Business occurs.

The vast majority of all that is communicated is nonverbal. Everything in nonverbal communication has a significant impact on you and me. Most people, however, live very randomly or live intentionally and then send messages they believe to say one thing but are received as something else.

And that is why so few people are influential. Almost no one communicates clearly. Misunderstandings abound.

Why?

People were never taught how to use the environment, their desks, the color of their homes, their jewelry, their necklines, skirt length, low rider pants, tattoos, and so forth to influence.

And when you think about it that is a shame because the words you and I say are darned important, but the nonverbal communication we send and receive is far more important.

Here you go: A woman in an office is hoping for attention—and a promotion—from superiors for the good job she's doing, so she starts with the sweater with a plunging neckline and so forth.

Attention?

She gets it.

Promotion?

Not a chance.

An accumulation of studies shows that women who are in the field of selling (not including casinos and resorts) have longer appointments with the decision maker if they dress revealingly.

The other result?

They make far fewer sales.

Dress is very influential.

The term body language is overused.

One person might say, "Her body language was very negative throughout the meeting," while another person might say, "His body language was very aggressive and intimidating." In both cases, however, body language is only a portion of the communication process that led to a specific conclusion or interpretation about the other person.

And interpretations are just as often incorrect as they are correct.

We speak of body language as if it were a separate, distinct activity, unrelated to other communication characteristics such as words, tone of voice, pacing, volume, and the like. The reality is all of these communication elements work together, and it is extremely difficult (if not impossible) to completely separate them from each other.

Despite the complex interrelationships involved in communication, researchers and scientists have successfully studied its parts and components to produce a much greater understanding of how these parts work individually and how they work together. Body language and other elements of nonverbal communication are components of communication that are readily observable and measurable, so our knowledge about them continues to grow at a steady and rapid pace.

This book sheds light on body language and nonverbal communication. The Secret Language of Business. And there is a great deal of information I am excited to present along the way.

You can use all the factors you learn about to be more influential. You can use everything you learn here to read other people.

Because people's body movements are typically controlled by the nonconscious mind, the person you are watching may not only not be aware of the message he is sending, he may not even cognitively agree with it!

(You probably want to read that again.)

One of the reasons there is so much trouble in communication in general is because people live on autopilot. We rarely use our conscious will. If we had to use conscious thought for everything we do, we'd never get anything done, and we'd all die in car accidents in the next week.

At the nonconscious level (the part of us that for better and worse "does" but doesn't "think") the brain sends impulses for the body to move, be still, look, engage, confront, run, hide, you name it.

And all of this happens before the thinking (cortical) part of the brain has clicked in and knows what the body is doing.

Words come out of your mouth and before you know it, you've said something you didn't mean (though you might have felt what you said).

Sometimes the thinking brain is in alignment with the nonconscious mind, and sometimes the two cause very different behaviors to happen.

In fact, a growing body of research reveals that *there is no significant correlation between the personality and behaviors of the nonconscious mind and the personality and behaviors of the conscious mind.*

(Say "wow.")

Thus, when you read someone, you might see one thing while the person is thinking of something totally different.

Finally, if you use this book to help you read the nonconscious mind and use the information as a way to predict nonconscious behavior and nonconscious decisions (those that happen quickly and without cognition) you will do much better at reading people and predicting their behavior.

You'll be able to influence people with ease.

You'll be able to know what they will do next more often than you might guess.

But will you know what they are thinking at the level of conscious thought?

That's not the best use of accurate body language reading.

One quick example.

Have you ever found yourself staring at someone, then after a minute you catch yourself and wonder why you are staring?

The person isn't attractive, and you aren't remotely interested.

But there you are burning a hole through this stranger.

In business you can get in big trouble for such behavior.

But try telling the woman that your nonconscious mind was at work and you didn't mean anything by it.

And of course, in this case, that is the truth!

Your nonconscious mind might have been staring because it perceived her as a threat, or because the woman looked like someone else who had some connection to you (typically emotional and not good) in the past.

Whatever the case (you can't be certain as to why the nonconscious mind directs the body to do something, you can only observe the result), you learned something and so did she, and they were not necessarily the same things.

More often than not The Secret Language of Business is about influencing the nonconscious mind and the behavior it directs.

That said, it's mighty important to influence the thinking brain, too.

As you read this book, always be aware of these two crucial distinctions.

People's thoughts and behaviors aren't related anywhere near as often as you'd like to believe.

As a rule, the conscious mind is more influenced by words and the nonconscious mind is more influenced by everything else (nonverbal communication, including body language).

To learn more about the nonconscious mind and the illusion of conscious will, there is a lengthy discussion at www.kevinhogan.com/nonconsciousmind.htm.

The Study of Nonverbal Communication

The observation and discussion of body language has been around in one form or another since the days of ancient Rome and Greece. Body language and nonverbal behavior is referenced in many varied disciplines, such as anthropology, dance, psychiatry, and sociology. Even Charles Darwin tackled the subject of facial expressions in 1872; many of his theories have since been proven by modern researchers.

Body language as a formal area of study first emerged in the post–World War II years. The 1950s saw the first few in-depth examinations of nonverbal communication and the 1960s saw an exponential growth in the number and type of formal studies. The discipline continued to grow and change in the 1970s, 1980s, and 1990s, with more growth and discovery happening in the current decade as well.

In the earliest years, researchers focused on body language as specific, separate actions with a single meaning. This gave way over the years to an understanding of body language as a complex aspect of communication where specific actions often have many different meanings depending on context, environment, culture, individual personalities, and so forth.

Why should you care about the formal study of body language?

Because the information revealed through scientific activities is enormously important to every aspect of your everyday life. There is no escaping the power and influence of body language; research and study simply identify and define it in ways that you can apply in the real world.

The problem until now has been a lack of resources to help you understand the scientific side of body language and translate it into practical applications for your life. This book is designed to fill that gap so you can look at nonverbal communication in an entirely new—and practical—way and then learn how to use that knowledge in an influential manner.

Before we get there, though, there are some basics to cover.

Nonverbal versus Verbal Communication

The definitions of nonverbal and verbal communication are of course argued from time to time as researchers gather more information and try to form the most precise descriptions possible. For the purposes of this book, though, I'll stick with the most basic, generally accepted definitions.

Nonverbal communication: The process of sending and receiving messages without using words. Examples include body language, facial expression, gesture, movement, touch, distance, eye contact, and so on.

Verbal communication: The process of sending and receiving messages using words. Examples include spoken words, written words, and sign language.

Wait a minute. Verbal communication includes the words you write down on a piece of paper? You probably learned somewhere along the line that verbal communication is only the *spoken* word, but the strict interpretation of verbal communication focuses on words in general—spoken, written, and signed.

Experts sometimes disagree about how to classify communication such as sign language and tone of voice. Sign language uses gestures, which is nonverbal, but those gestures are actually words, which is verbal. Tone of voice is a spoken sound, which is verbal, but it is not a word so it is nonverbal.

It's easy to see how and why there are so many different interpretations, definitions, and nuances when it comes to discussing nonverbal and verbal communication. I'll leave it to the academic and scientific experts to figure out the finer points and move on to the more practical aspects of body language. My goal is to help you understand The Secret Language of Business.

Does one of these sentences include nonverbal communication?

1. It doesn't make any difference whether we categorize written material as verbal or nonverbal communication.

2. It DOESN'T make ANY DIFFERENCE whether we categorize written material as verbal or nonverbal communication!

Answer?

I don't know . . .

How Body Language Influences Communication

In an earlier section, I stated that nonverbal and verbal elements of communication couldn't be completely separated and isolated from the overall communication process. This is one of the most interesting (and at times frustrating) aspects of studying communication, because the potential variations and interactions are so numerous and so diverse that it can be hard to categorize them in a meaningful, definite way.

When you think solely about body language and how it influences communication, though, some basic features and functions emerge. These fall into the following general categories as identified by Mark Knapp in his book *Nonverbal Communication in Human Interaction*:

- Repeating
- Conflicting
- Complementing
- Substituting
- Accenting/Moderating
- Regulating

Those are forbidding-sounding categories that come straight from the scientific and academic world. Let's give them some better real-world meaning with a few examples.

Repeating: Nonverbal behavior often serves to repeat what is said verbally. When you ask your spouse to put down the bag of groceries on the table, do you point to the table during or after you speak? If so, that's repeating. The act of pointing (nonverbal) repeats the request (verbal) of where to put the groceries.

Conflicting: This is one of the biggest and most varied categories of nonverbal behavior. When you tell your friend the cake she baked is delicious (verbal) but your eyes dart away (nonverbal), that's conflicting. Conflicting body language is a bright, flashing indicator when you lie, feel nervous, disagree, or otherwise feel trapped or ambivalent about something. When verbal and nonverbal elements are in conflict, the person receiving the communication will usually give more credibility to the nonverbal behavior.

Even more fascinating, though, is that we interpret conflicting information based in part on how easy or hard it is to fake the particular nonverbal behavior. For instance, a child might say she has a stomachache and is unable to take out the garbage. The body language of a stomachache is hard to fake—pale color, clammy skin, and perhaps a fever or general discomfort for an extended period of time. Most parents will be skeptical from the start, only starting to believe her when it becomes clear her nonverbal behaviors are real.

Complementing: This category is somewhat intertwined with the Conflicting category. Nonverbal behavior that complements and supports verbal statements lends credibility to those statements if the nonverbal behavior is perceived to be genuine and not faked. For instance, I knew a woman who was pulled over by a state patrol officer for speeding. She was genuinely embarrassed at being pulled over because she had simply not paid attention to her speed. To make things worse, in nearly 20 years of driving, she had never been pulled over before. By the time the officer got to her car she was crying and very upset with herself.

Now, police officers are especially good at reading verbal and nonverbal communication under stress, because let's face it, the people they encounter don't want to get a ticket or go to jail so they will often try to lie and talk their way out of the situation. The state patrol officer who pulled over my friend could see right away that her nonverbal behavior (crying, shaking, and so on) was real and not faked. This, coupled with her immaculate driving record and admission of wrongdoing, convinced him to let her go with a warning. Her nonverbal behavior complemented her verbal statements, thus making them more credible to the officer.

Substituting: This category is for the body language used when a person does not want to use verbal communication. Perhaps the words are too hard to say out loud or saying them would create a conflict or confrontation. In this kind of situation, substituting nonverbal behavior for the words can get the message across in a way that is more comfortable.

Have you ever encountered an acquaintance in the grocery store who starts talking and then keeps talking? When that happens, chances are you first try to disengage yourself from the conversation using body language. You might start glancing away from the other person, or perhaps turn your body and/or take a step or two away. If the other person does not get the message you might have to resort to saying "I have to go now" or something similar, but you'd rather not have to do that. You would rather substitute nonverbal communication to end the conversation.

Accenting/Moderating: This category captures the kinds of nonverbal communication designed to enhance a verbal message. It might serve to amplify a particular point and give it more emphasis, or it might serve to moderate or soften a particular point. Either way, this type of body language adds depth and nuance to a message.

For instance, if you are angry with a coworker you might accent the message with a pointing gesture, a frown, and a shake of your head. This lets the other person know you are quite serious about your anger and want them to get the message very clearly. If you are correcting a minor mistake made by an employee, however, you might moderate the message with a palm up gesture, a reassuring smile, or a pat on the shoulder for encouragement. This lets the other person know you are serious about wanting the mistake corrected, but also softens the message a bit so he or she understands it's not the end of the world, just a mistake and a learning experience.

Regulating: This category contains nonverbal behaviors that regulate or pace the communication of a message. It might be used to indicate when you are ready to move from one topic to another topic, or to transition smoothly to another person's chance to speak. Regulating behaviors help to moderate and control the communication between and among multiple people.

For instance, if you are leading the roundtable segment of a team meeting, you might nod, turn, and gesture to the next person at the table when it is his or her turn to speak. Some people are not very good at regulating behaviors; they interrupt before another person is finished speaking, or they talk constantly without allowing input from others.

Practical Applications of Body Language

So what does this all really mean? What are the practical applications of body language and nonverbal communication? The practical applications are nearly limitless, and quite often they are used unconsciously rather than deliberately. Some people are just naturals when it comes to the effective use of body language in everyday life, while others struggle with how to learn it and use it well.

Common examples of when and where nonverbal communication applies to the real world include:

- Office
- Selling
- Negotiations
- Job interviews
- Persuasive discussions
- Client/vendor interactions
- Walking through the grocery store
- Meetings
- Politics
- Hiring
- Intimacy
- Friendship
- Parenting
- Working with animals
- Business meetings
- Real estate showings
- Meal time
- Running errands
- Parent-teacher conferences
- Shopping
- Group leadership
- Sports activities
- Vacation planning

This list could go on and on and on! The reality is that nonverbal communication is part of everything you do every day.

Your personal nonverbal communication influences everyone around you . . . and theirs influences you.

There is no way to avoid it—and why would you want to? Body language is one of the most powerful components of the communication process, and you have the choice of how you use it. You can leave it to your unconscious or actively learn to apply it.

Choose the more active path of learning because that holds the greatest potential for making all aspects of your life richer, more interesting, more productive, and more effective. Helping you to do that is why I wrote this book.

Chapter 1 TAKEAWAYS

1. The observation and discussion of body language has been around for centuries but only became a serious scientific discipline after the end of World War II.

2. Body language is an important component of the overall communication process, but cannot be entirely separated and isolated from other components. They all integrate and interact with each other in many different ways, depending on context, environment, culture, personalities, and so forth.

3. There are many detailed, nuanced definitions that may be applied to nonverbal communication and verbal communication, but for the purposes of this book we'll focus on the most basic definitions:

    Nonverbal communication. The process of sending and receiving messages without using words. Examples include body language, facial expression, gesture, movement, touch, distance, eye contact, and the like.

    Verbal communication. The process of sending and receiving messages using words. Examples include spoken words, written words, and sign language.

4. There are six main categories of body language, as discussed in *Nonverbal Communication in Human Interaction* by Mark Knapp:

- Repeating
- Conflicting
- Complementing
- Substituting
- Accenting/Moderating
- Regulating

5. Body language has nearly endless practical applications in everyday life, whether it is applied unconsciously or with conscious deliberation. The best and most effective communicators take an active interest in learning how to make the best use of nonverbal communication.

Read more about the nonconscious mind and how it is often confused with the unconscious or subconscious mind at www .kevinhogan.com/nonconsciousmind.htm.

Chapter 1 WORKSHEET

---

1. Review the Chapter 1 Takeaways and answer the following:

- Which key point(s) did you find most interesting? Why?
- Which key point(s) did you find most surprising? Why?

2. Think about a recent example of communication you had with another person. Write down a description of the nonverbal behaviors that occurred during the interaction.

Now categorize each nonverbal behavior (repeating, conflicting, complementing, substituting, accenting/moderating, or regulating).

3. Go to a restaurant, coffee shop, shopping mall, or other public location and observe an interaction between two or more people. Write down a description of the nonverbal behaviors you observe.

    Now categorize each nonverbal behavior (repeating, conflicting, complementing, substituting, accenting/moderating, or regulating).

2

The Power of the Secret Language of Business

I t is difficult to overestimate the power of body language. Those who pretend to be experts throw around figures such as 75 percent, 85 percent, even 90 percent when they try to define how much of a message is communicated nonverbally rather than verbally. It actually differs from context to context and individual to individual. There is no fixed number or even an average. The bottom line is the power of even the very best verbal communication pales in comparison to the power of body language and nonverbal communication.

Why Should You Care about Body Language?

Stinky people.

They bother me.

I confess it, here and now.

I'm "smell sensitive."

I can tell someone what they had for lunch, whether they had alcohol, were near a cigarette, and whether I can stay within meters of them because of their body's scent.

So at the conscious and probably nonconscious level you and I are aware to a greater or lesser degree of scent, and it causes us to form opinions about people.

But sometimes all of this happens at the nonconscious level...

...and sometimes the result of scientific research is a little scary.

Research shows that <u>females are far more attracted to males with other females' scents on them</u>.

Notice that it is not the scent of perfume, which obviously covers scent, but *the scent of another female.*

It appears that evolution has supplied females a yardstick with which to measure males. Females have an olfactory sensitivity about 10 times that of males in terms of sexuality and pheromones.

Evolution determines that females instinctively seek a fertile partner with good genes and by virtue of having another woman's scent on him, the male has been already been "tested and approved."

And *all* of this happens at the nonconscious level.

If you communicate to earn a living you must obviously master nonverbal communication.

I sometimes come across people during my events who doubt the influence of body language or simply don't believe it is such an important part of life. They usually agree it is important when giving formal presentations and the like, but when it comes to daily activities it is something that's just there in the background. Often these people attend the seminar because their boss is making them go, or they feel they have to attend as part of their career development plan. In other words, they are physically present but not necessarily mentally or emotionally engaged in the process.

When I meet someone who holds this opinion I like to go through a quick but powerful exercise. I ask the person to list at least five things she has done that day, promising to show her how body language affected each activity. I write each activity on a separate piece of flip chart paper, leaving plenty of room on the paper for later on in the exercise.

Here's a typical list from a body language skeptic:

1. I woke up.
2. I ate breakfast.
3. I drove to the post office.
4. I stopped to pick up coffee.
5. I came to this body language seminar.

This list is usually accompanied by a somewhat smug expression, almost daring me to find anything related to body language in the daily, mundane activities of life. Imagine the surprise, then, when I start down responding to the list, making notes on each flip chart sheet that look something like this:

1. **You woke up.** When the alarm went off you may have grimaced, given a heavy and dejected sigh, sat up with shoulders slumped and head hanging down. All of those nonverbal behaviors influenced your own attitude and feelings about waking up. If there was another person in the room, your nonverbal behaviors influenced his or her impression of you, expectations for interacting with you, and his or her own attitude toward getting out of bed.

2. **You ate breakfast.** You walked into the kitchen with a certain posture and body movement. It may have been upright and eyes looking forward or it may have been hunched over and eyes looking down. As you ate breakfast, you might have sat with shoulders slumped or with shoulders held back. Maybe you were focused on the newspaper, ignoring the cat or dog trying to attract your attention. If there were other people in the room, a slumped posture and focus on the newspaper would have made them reluctant to speak with you; an upright posture, eye contact, and pleasant facial expression would have made them eager to speak with you.

3. **You drove to the post office.** You turned the car onto the street and began driving, both hands firmly on the wheel and eyes focused on the road. Other drivers caught a glimpse of your posture and focus, immediately forming an opinion about what actions to expect from you as you drove past. Or, you might have sat slumped back, one elbow on the center armrest, head tilted slightly to one side as if daydreaming or thinking about something else. Perhaps you were talking on your cell phone, smiling pleasantly or with a stern look on your face. When you arrived at the post office, you got out of the car and slammed the door and walked directly into the building. Others nearby observed this behavior and made an instant judgment about your attitude and what they might expect if they were to interact with you. If there was another person in the car with you during the drive, your nonverbal behaviors influenced his willingness to talk to you, his feelings of safety, and his sense of whether or not you were happy to have him in the car with you.

4. **You stopped to pick up coffee.** You drove up to the coffee stand and rolled down your window. You looked up, made eye contact, smiled, and said good morning. The person behind the counter greeted you back with a friendly smile and sincere hello. She judged you a nice person and turned to make your coffee, perhaps with a bit more care because you have made a positive impression. On the other hand, you may have arrived at the coffee stand with a stern facial expression. When the server greeted you, you didn't smile back or exchange greetings; you placed your order and turned your head in a way that appeared dismissive. You did not make a very positive impression, and the person behind the counter judged you to be grumpy. Her most immediate goal is to make your coffee, collect the money, and get you out of there.

5. **You came to this body language seminar.** You walked into the seminar room and looked for a place to sit. You walked slowly, almost casually, with a bored or stern look on your face because you really didn't want to be here. You chose a seat in the back of the room so you could be physically present but avoid any active involvement. The use of round tables rather than rows of chairs worried you because you might have to interact with others at the table, so you picked a table that was empty and spread out your things. Your head was down with an expression of concentration on your face sending the message that you were busy and not interested in chatting or being enthusiastic about the seminar. Or perhaps you walked into the room with an upright posture and a confident stride. You paused to look around, smiling and greeting people who walked past you. Your eyes scanned the room, making eye contact with various people, and you selected a seat near the front. You reached out to shake hands with others at the table, introducing yourself with a smile and a nod of the head. You placed your things nearby but not blocking you, and made eye contact with the people around you. You chatted a bit, nodding your head, leaning forward, smiling, and using a variety of facial expressions during the conversation.

By the time I get to the end of the list, everyone in the room is paying attention. Some nod their heads in a wise way, as if to say, "Yup, I already knew all of that," while others laugh nervously or self-consciously, recognizing themselves in the examples just given and feeling glad they were not the one whose morning activities were discussed.

Now, getting back to the original question at the beginning of this section—why should you care about body language? Because body language is a major part of communication and you are constantly communicating, so when your body language becomes more effective your communication does as well and you begin to influence in the direction of *choice* and not randomness.

The rest of this chapter will look closely at the three key communication roles we all play—sender, receiver, and observer. Body language and nonverbal behaviors affect all of these roles in a great number of ways, so it's worth spending some extra time going into them in a more detailed manner.

When You Are the Sender

When you are the sender of a message, your body language is an amazing mix of behaviors. Your behaviors can shift rapidly at times, slowly at other times, but they are always there in one form or another. A sender's body language is generally categorized as either conscious or nonconscious, but I like to use the words deliberate and spontaneous instead. These words do a much better job of capturing the nature of certain behaviors and how they appear in your daily life.

Deliberate body language. You consciously choose these behaviors because they serve a specific purpose. For instance, when you walk into a room for a job interview, you hold yourself in an upright posture, smile, shake hands, and introduce yourself to others in the room. Somewhere along the line, you were taught these are the nonverbal behaviors that express your professionalism, enthusiasm, and openness. There are people who seem to just naturally exhibit these behaviors without being taught, but regardless of your existing natural tendencies, it is very likely you will choose to emphasize them in an interview situation.

Another great example of deliberate body language occurs every year during the Academy Awards in Hollywood. For each award, the presenter reads the names of the nominees and the TV cameras focus in on each of them. When the winner's name is read the other nominees continue smiling, and they applaud and may even nod their head in agreement with the choice made by the judges. These are all deliberate, nonverbal behaviors, designed to cover up their own disappointment and to show them behaving in a socially appropriate way. It might feel good to grimace, pout, or stomp out in a huff, but those are not considered polite behaviors so each non-winner makes a conscious effort to use appropriate body language.

What about in your everyday life? What kinds of deliberate body language do you use? Here are a few examples I have heard in my seminars and workshops:

- If you are moving into line at the grocery store checkout counter and another person is approaching at the same time, avoid eye contact with that person and walk confidently into line so you end up ahead of her instead of behind her.

- Avoid eye contact and move away from the boss if you're late with a task or project.

- A new teacher walks into his classroom on the first day of school with confidence and a calm demeanor, despite feeling terrified.

- You smile, shake hands, and politely say hello when your ex-girlfriend introduces you to her new boyfriend.

- When disciplining a child, stay standing while the child stays seated. This higher position gives you added authority.

- Your take your son along with you to a dental appointment, and, although you are very nervous about the root canal the dentist is about to perform, you smile and act confident to set a good example for your son.

- You hate broccoli with a passion, but when you arrive at your boyfriend's home to have dinner with his parents for the first time, you discover the main dish is broccoli casserole. Despite your inner feelings, you eat the casserole with your head nodding approval, your eyes closed in enjoyment, and your face set in a smile when his mother offers to give you the recipe.

- It's 3 A.M., and your dogs wake up whining to go outside. You lay completely still, making a deliberate effort to breathe deeply and steadily so it appears you are still asleep. After a few minutes of this, your spouse grumbles, throws back the covers, and takes the dogs to the back door.

I'm continually amazed at the creative and interesting examples brought up during seminars. Just when I think I've heard every possible example there could be, someone comes up with something entirely new to add to my list.

Reading Some Sending Samples
Women read signals from men in ways that most men would not.

Women look at the condition of the inside of a man's car. Specifically, are the front and back seats clean?

Women expect men to be on time, and they lose brownie points when they are not.

Women do not want to be gazed at by men whose eyes are above their eye level if the women have no sexual interest in the men.

So far, I've talked about deliberate body language in terms of nonverbal behaviors you choose to use as part of your communication, but there is another side to this you should understand. There are times when deliberate body language consists of no action or behavior at all. Your choice to avoid showing a behavior is a deliberate behavior all on its own.

If you have ever worked in an office filled with cubicles you'll probably understand this one right away.

A coworker walks down the aisle making an announcement that her daughter is selling wrapping paper as a school fundraiser. She is waving the order form around, looking for eye contact or some indication of interest. You make the deliberate choice to keep working along, staying seated and with your eyes on your computer. You don't even turn your head to glance at her because you don't want to say "no" right to her face (and you can't slap her because you'd get written up).

Here's another one, straight from the real-world experience of most parents. Your son and daughter are in the kitchen arguing over something minor, while you're in the living room reading. The argument continues and you think about intervening to help resolve the situation so you can get back to reading in peace and quiet, but you decide to let them sort it out for themselves. You continue reading, not turning your head to look or listen, not appearing to even notice there is an argument going on right in the next room. There is no noticeable change in your body language, but because it is due to a conscious choice, your lack of behavior is an example of deliberate body language.

Spontaneous body language. These behaviors occur automatically and unintentionally. For instance, when you are startled by a scary scene in a movie you gasp, jump back a little, and your facial expression turns to fear. These behaviors may only last for a few seconds, but they are very real nonetheless. What's more, they influence your view of yourself and others' views of you as well.

It is possible to learn how to minimize and even control spontaneous behaviors, but it takes time and practice. Your personality type has a strong influence on how easily and how well you handle these behaviors, too. If you are very outgoing, expressive, and extroverted then you are naturally freer with your spontaneous body language and will have a tougher time learning to manage it. If you are reserved, introverted, and tend to internalize, you are naturally more controlled with your spontaneous body language and will probably have a much easier time learning to manage it.

Children, teenagers, and young adults tend to show the most spontaneous nonverbal behaviors because they are less practiced at hiding and covering them up. They have not yet been fully indoctrinated by society and its expectations for what is and isn't appropriate. For instance, children who see an adult with a large scar or facial disfigurement are likely to spontaneously pull back, grimace, and point. They don't mean to be rude or disrespectful, they simply haven't learned how to mask and manage those spontaneous nonverbal behaviors that might be hurtful or embarrassing to someone else.

Over time and with experience, most people learn to manage all but the most intense spontaneous behaviors. You might have learned to avoid crying when you miss out on a promotion, but if a friend, relative, or beloved pet dies then the tears are likely to come pouring out all on their own. The body language associated with anger is another area where most people learn to mask their behaviors unless the anger is overwhelming in some way.

One interesting aspect of spontaneous body language is that these behaviors are often faked in an attempt to gain attention or advantage. An obvious example is a teenage girl who pretends to be startled by a boy whom she likes as a way to get him to notice her. Another is an adult who might pretend to be surprised when given an award of some sort as a way of appearing humble.

There is a real irony in all of this, of course. When you fake a spontaneous nonverbal behavior, it becomes a deliberate nonverbal behavior, so it technically belongs in the previous section of this chapter.

When You Are the Receiver

When you are the receiver of a message, body language plays an important role in two major ways—your own nonverbal behaviors and your interpretation of the sender's nonverbal behaviors. In other words, the receiver has to simultaneously take in the sender's message, engage in his own deliberate and/or spontaneous body language, and interpret the sender's body language. All of this occurs in just a few seconds or less, and what's more, it occurs continuously throughout the interaction.

As I describe this process in a seminar environment, it's amazing to watch the faces and behaviors of participants as the complexity of it all sinks in. They start to catch a glimpse of just how ingrained body language is throughout every aspect of our lives. It becomes even more interesting when I ask people to give me an analogy that accurately describes the process.

My own personal favorite is the analogy of two jugglers tossing oranges back and forth to each other. Each juggler is focused on keeping his own oranges in the air, throwing extra oranges to the other juggler, and catching the oranges thrown to him by the other juggler.

Now, let's get back to the receiver portion of an interaction. When you are on the receiving end of a message, you are literally processing hundreds (if not thousands) of bits of information all at once, so your brain is forced to do a lot of that processing unconsciously. You simply couldn't handle the huge flow of information otherwise.

If you have been trained in nonverbal communication your unconscious mind processes that information instantly and spits out the answers you need.

If you've been guessing or judging behaviors and not checking to see if you were right (like 99.99 percent of people on this planet) you'll find your instincts are wrong far more often than they are right.

Problem is, we rarely see where we are wrong, because we are always looking to find where we are right about stuff, and that is why we think we are good at reading body language when in truth, our failure to do so has cost us millions of dollars and ruined relationships to boot.

It turns out that nonverbal information is processed almost entirely in the unconscious mind. Human beings are extremely sensitive to nonverbal communication, so much so that you can make a decision about the body language you see but not be able to identify exactly which parts of that language led you to your final conclusion.

Some people tend to be more sensitive to body language than others, most notably women.

It may sound sexist or reverse sexist if there is such a thing, but it's not; the scientific research is rock solid. Most experts think the gender difference is based in nature, in part because women are traditionally most responsible for infant care and an infant's primary form of communication is nonverbal. Of course, this is not the entire story, but it is an interesting part of it.

Regardless of your gender, receiving requires you to make judgments about the message, such as:

- Is it truthful?
- Is it sincere?
- Is it accurate?
- Is it urgent?
- Is it important?
- Is it complete?

Receiving also requires you to make judgments about the sender, such as:

- Is he hiding something?
- Is she trying to manipulate me?
- Is he encouraging me?
- Is she angry?
- Is he trying to avoid a sensitive topic?
- Is she trying to intimidate me?

When you are the receiver, your interpretation of a message is based on many things—words, experience, personality, previous interactions, and so on—but body language is thought to be one of the most influential factors in your interpretation.

When You Are the Observer

When you are the observer, the body language component of communication takes on entirely new dimensions. You are not directly involved in the communication interaction so observation of body language and nonverbal behaviors becomes even more critical to interpreting what is happening.

Observation is not objective, however. You bring your own likes, dislikes, biases, experiences, and personal qualities to every observation opportunity, as do all of the other observers of a particular interaction. This explains why several people can observe the same event and walk away with completely different accounts of the event.

Here's an example of how this happens. Let's say you are a very reserved, introverted person. You are not prone to expressing your emotions and your body language is nearly always controlled and conservative. One afternoon you walk into your office and observe a discussion between two people, Joe and Jim.

Joe is very expressive and extroverted, while Jim is reserved and introverted. Joe and Jim have an energetic conversation about a difficult subject, and they are unable to reach an acceptable agreement between them. Later on, your manager asks you what happened between Joe and Jim.

From your perspective as a reserved person, you may interpret Joe's expressive body language as being angry, emotional, or otherwise too extreme for the situation. On the other hand, you may interpret Jim's reserved body language as being calm, reasonable, and controlled. Another person who is more expressive would probably have an entirely different interpretation of the interaction between Joe and Jim.

Even your mood has a powerful impact on observation and interpretation of communication interactions. If you are in a bad mood and feeling negative, you are much more likely to interpret others as having that same kind of bad mood and negative feelings. What if you are in a happy, positive mood? You guessed it. Your interpretations are much more likely to perceive happiness and a positive mood in the body language and nonverbal behaviors of others.

Another factor in your interpretations as an observer is the relationship you have with the person or people you observe. You will naturally tend to observe and interpret the body language of a close friend or family member with entirely different criteria than you would if observing a stranger, new acquaintance, or someone whom you strongly dislike.

Now, I'm not saying you are not a trustworthy observer just because you have your own perceptions, personality, moods, and relationships. You are a human being so there is no way to be 100 percent unbiased and objective about anything. What I want you to think about is how your own communication characteristics influence your interpretation of others' body language, and the effect it has on your judgments about a message, a sender, a receiver, or any combination of these. Awareness is the most important step toward choosing thoughtful observation rather than simply relying on gut reaction and unconscious interpretations.

Astonishing Body Language Facts

The Finger Factor

You may not need your entire body to evaluate some general tendencies you might possess.

Look at your right hand and note the length of your index finger compared with the ring finger.

(*continued*)

Astonishing Body Language Facts (*Continued*)

Most women (female pattern) have the fingers almost exactly the same length.

Most men (male pattern) have a shorter index finger.

Male pattern is more likely to be good at math.

Men with male pattern are more likely to be physically aggressive throughout life.

Homosexual women tend to have a male pattern hand.

Men with older brothers have a more masculine finger length pattern than men without older brothers.

Men with more feminine finger ratios are more prone to depression.

Children with longer ring fingers compared to index fingers are likely to have higher math scores than literacy or verbal scores on the SAT college entrance exam.

Students with the reverse finger-length ratio are likely to have higher reading and writing, or verbal scores versus math scores.

Finally, all of these facts are on average. They are one piece of information you now have that you didn't when you bought this book.

Chapter 2 **TAKEAWAYS**

1. Body language and nonverbal behaviors are the most powerful part of the communication process. Most people don't realize just how powerful they truly are until they take a fresh look at their own body language during even the most mundane daily activities.

2. When you are the sender of a message, your body language is a complex mix of behaviors. They can generally be

categorized as either deliberate (conscious) or spontaneous (unconscious).

3. Deliberate body language can take the form of choosing a particular action or choosing not to take action at all. Spontaneous body language is automatic and unintentional. Learning to control it and manage it for different situations and social norms requires time and experience.

4. Children, teenagers, and young adults tend to exhibit the most spontaneous nonverbal behaviors; this is primarily due to their relative youth and lack of life experiences. Adults who are expressive and extroverted tend to exhibit more spontaneous body language than do adults who are reserved and introverted.

5. When you are the receiver of a message, body language plays an important role. You interpret the sender's nonverbal behaviors and manage your own nonverbal behaviors. Receiving requires the processing of large amounts of information, so your brain handles most of it unconsciously. As the receiver, you make judgments about the message itself as well as about the sender.

6. When you are the observer, you rely even more on body language and nonverbal behaviors to interpret an interaction. Your own tendencies (expressive vs. reserved) influence your interpretations, as do many other things such as your mood, your personality, and your relationship with the observed participants.

Chapter 2 **WORKSHEET**

---

1. Review the Chapter 2 Takeaways and answer the following:
   - Which key point(s) did you find most interesting? Why?
   - Which key point(s) did you find most surprising? Why?

2. Imagine you are a body language skeptic. Write down three to five activities you have done today, and then write down all of the ways body language and nonverbal behaviors influenced those activities.

3. Think about a communication interaction where you were the sender. Write down the body language and nonverbal behaviors you used, and note which ones were deliberate and which ones were spontaneous.

4. Think about a communication interaction where you were the receiver. Write down the body language and nonverbal behaviors you processed, and then note how you interpreted the message and how you interpreted the sender.

5. Think about a communication interaction where you were the observer. How did your own personality, perceptions, mood, and personal relationships influence your observations and interpretations?

3

Elements of Body Language

There are worksheets at www.kevinhogan.com/worksheets.htm that you can print out and use forever. (You can use them before sales presentations, meetings, and events where you are speaking. In addition, you can use one chart *during* meetings to give you an edge that you've never experienced before.)

The elements of body language can be broken down in many ways, from physical body parts to how those body parts are used. Academics and scientists can spend years studying just a single element, and entire books have been written on each of the eight elements you'll learn about in this chapter.

My purpose here is to expand your understanding of body language by breaking it down into the key elements—eyes, face, gestures, touch, posture, movement, appearance, and voice. Each one plays an important role in nonverbal behavior, but as you've come to expect with body language, none of them operate in complete isolation. They work together, often in very subtle ways, and different combinations can produce entirely different body language messages. You will benefit greatly by keeping this in mind as you read through the chapter.

Eyes

The eyes are the windows to the soul, it has been said, and most people would say this is indeed true. Your eyes have a huge impact on communication and are a key component of your body language. Eye movement and use is often the first nonverbal behavior others notice because your eyes are usually the first place they look and the place they come back to the most often.

Your eyes are powerful nonverbal tools in part because you can make conscious choices of how to use them and in part, because they do a lot of things completely on their own. This combination of deliberate and spontaneous body language is quite interesting and influential.

The deliberate movements of your eyes communicate a great deal to other people. You've no doubt been taught to make regular eye contact with an audience when making a presentation, but the benefits of that eye contact can rapidly disappear if your eyes move too quickly from person to person. A steady, confident gaze becomes a nervous darting of the eyes if you don't strike the right balance between individual eye contact and working the room.

The length and intensity of your eye contact sends some very specific messages. For instance, when meeting someone for the first time it is considered polite to make eye contact for a few seconds but it is considered quite rude to make eye contact and stare. In an intimate setting such as a date, though, an extended gaze is a sign of interest, attention, and affection. And what if you're in a shopping mall?

Brief eye contact is considered normal but outright staring at other people is often interpreted as hostile or threatening.

(Or just weird.)

Not making eye contact is just as powerful. You might break eye contact and look away as a signal to the other person you are ready to end the conversation, are bored with the subject of the conversation, or are frustrated that the other person is talking too much. Looking away can also be a sign of submission; women tend to do this a lot during the first few interactions with someone whom they find attractive. The most intense form of not making eye contact is deliberately looking past or away from someone who is obviously trying to get your attention. This may be interpreted as dominance, dismissal, or just plain rudeness.

Where you direct your gaze is a strong nonverbal behavior as well. The classic example, of course, is a man who spends more time looking at a woman's chest than at her face, but there are other examples. For instance, if you are speaking with someone who has a facial scar or birthmark, you might find yourself looking at that rather than the person's eyes. This is a perfectly normal tendency, but society teaches that it is rude. Children haven't absorbed this lesson fully so they will openly stare at anything they find unusual such as a physical disability, unusual clothing, and the like.

The spontaneous body language of your eyes is a bit more subtle but just as powerful. You know your eyes dilate and contract based on the brightness of light around you, but you might not know they also change noticeably based on your mood, attitude, and emotions.

What's more, they make these changes on their own and outside of your conscious control. The actions of your pupils are extremely noticeable, furthermore, because so much of human behavior is based around eye contact and the face.

Your pupils contract noticeably when you are angry, unhappy, or perceiving something as negative or suspicious. They dilate noticeably when you are excited, happy, aroused, or even when your brain is engaged in problem-solving activity. All of these actions occur spontaneously, outside of your control, but it's also interesting to note that the way others interpret these actions is also spontaneous and automatic.

For instance, if you are speaking with someone whose pupils contract you will start to perceive that person as angry or unhappy. If I then ask how you came to that conclusion, you would probably have trouble pinpointing exactly how you did it. You might mention some other nonverbal behavior, but the truth is pupil contraction is the trigger to your interpretation.

Human beings tend to interpret dilated pupils as more attractive than contracted pupils. This is an integral part of human intimacy and interaction. For instance, when two people are attracted to each other their pupils dilate in response to their feelings.

Babies' pupils dilate whenever another human being—especially their mothers—is nearby to entice that other person to feel affection and caring. It is not deliberate, of course, but a characteristic that is considered part of the survival mechanism.

Do you tend to notice people with light colored eyes more quickly than people with dark colored eyes? There is a reason for that. The contrast between the pupil and a light colored eye is much sharper than between the pupil and a dark colored eye, so you are naturally drawn to the more noticeable contrast. This is one reason why people with light colored eyes create such a stir in cultures where the population is primarily dark eyed. The novelty and intensity of contrast between pupil and eye color draws a lot of attention and interest.

The attractiveness of dilated pupils plays an important role in advertising as well. Look at any picture of a model and you'll see that his or her pupils are dilated; this is especially true in ads for makeup or facial care products. The effect of dilation is so strong, in fact, that advertisers will touch up photos to increase the size of the model's pupils in the final version of the photo.

You and I like big pupils . . . the bigger the better.

What about blinking?

It is primarily a spontaneous nonverbal behavior, although it can become deliberate if you focus on it. The speed and frequency of blinking sends a body language message ranging from nervousness to deception to stress to superiority, depending on the context. For instance, if you are speaking with someone who sees you as inferior, that person's blinks may be slightly slower than normal. This keeps their eyes covered longer in an unconscious attempt to block you from their sight. In extreme instances, the person might talk for several seconds at a time with eyes closed. This is usually accompanied by a backward tilt of the head, allowing the person to effectively look down at you.

Rule of thumb: Increased rate of blinking is correlated to increased anxiety and/or deception . . . unless their contact lens is bothering them.

Want to send a "liking message" with your eyes?

Use everything I've talked about in this section and mix this in the recipe as well: When breaking eye contact, don't look from side to side, at other people or things, or up. Only look down, defocused, and then bring your eyes back up to meet the other person.

The strength of this message can be as disarming as a tornado. Why?

No one uses it and it's filled with respect, appreciation, and liking.

Face

Many experts consider facial expressions the most important nonverbal behavior of all. Your face is the focal point of conversation and interaction, so the impact of its movements and expressions is magnified. The face is a tool for communicating emotions and feelings, but it is also important for regulating and directing an interaction.

Let's say you are interacting with another person and you want to say something. If the other person is already talking, your facial expression will change to indicate you want a turn. Your eyebrows rise slightly, and your mouth opens as if you are about to speak. Smiling is a facial expression used when listening to someone else as a way of encouraging them, acknowledging what they are saying, and signaling you are interested in what they are saying.

Facial expressions can communicate nearly any emotion you want, the most common being happiness, fear, disgust, anger, sadness, and surprise. They typically appear as follows:

- Happiness—Lips pull back and up at the corners; cheeks raise up; so-called crow's feet wrinkles become noticeable on the outside of the eyes.

- Fear—Mouth opens slightly; lips are tense; eyebrows rise up and together; forehead wrinkles in the center; upper eyelid rises up.

- Disgust—Nose wrinkles up; cheeks raise up; eyebrows lower; upper lip rises up; lower lip may be raised up against the upper lip or lowered slightly and pushed out.

- Anger—Eyes stare with contracted pupils, perhaps seeming to bulge out; eyebrows lower, coming together and creating wrinkles between them; lips may be tense and pressed together or tense and open.

- Sadness—Lips draw down in the corners, perhaps trembling; eyebrows rise up slightly; upper eyelid rises up in the inner corner.

- Surprise—Eyelids open wide; eyebrows arch up; wrinkles appear across entire forehead; jaw drops and mouth opens.

Your face is a useful flirtation device. (It's like a flotation device on an airplane . . . okay, maybe not.)

A smile, a wink, and raised eyebrows in the right social situation can attract another person's attention and communicate interest. Once a conversation is started, these same facial expressions help to encourage further interest and interaction. The power of facial expression for attracting and engaging someone else is so big that it can become a misused tool for manipulating or otherwise influencing another person.

There are cultural differences in how facial body language is interpreted as well. For instance, Americans tend to read more emotion into the face than do Japanese. Americans put their focus on the mouth when trying to understand what someone is saying. The Japanese put their attention on the eyes.

People from the same culture are more accurate in reading each others' facial expressions, a finding you would expect, of course.

Facial expression can be either deliberate or spontaneous depending on the person and the situation. Children tend to show their facial expressions spontaneously, with little or no deliberate control. Adults, on the other hand, have learned through the years to mask or control certain facial expressions in certain situations where they are considered inappropriate or unwise.

Want People to Feel as if You Are Both on the Same Wavelength?

Allow yourself to become infected by their emotional output. In other words, if you see them get excited because the home team got a touchdown, make sure you get caught up in that excitement as well, and, make sure they see that.

If your counterpart is angry, allow your face to come close to matching his emotional intensity.

These kind of near matches really build empathy and liking between two people or groups of people.

However, don't match the exact level of excitement or anger. This can often backfire as being seen as dramatic not genuine, and an overall bad idea.

Gestures

Gestures are commonly recognized as movements used to communicate a message or enhance the communication of a message. Unlike other elements of body language, to be considered a true gesture the

movement must be deliberate and intentional. For instance, if you
stand up to walk across the room that is a movement, but it is not
a gesture. If you walk across the room in an exaggerated way, such
as on your toes, skipping, taking especially large steps, and so forth,
then it is considered a gesture. Your choice to exaggerate the walk is a
deliberate action for the purpose of communicating or enhancing the
communication of your message.

**Want to Make Sure They Don't Engage You in Conversation
as You Leave Your Office?**

As soon as you get to your door, increase your stride length and
pace. Focus your eyes far in front of you so you don't make eye
contact with the people you walk past. If you do accidentally
make eye contact make sure you smile at the person and keep
walking.

There are two generally recognized categories of gestures:

1. Speech-independent gestures.
2. Speech-related gestures.

Gestures are especially noteworthy because they are the type of
nonverbal communication that is most likely to differ from culture to
culture. Speech-independent gestures are most likely to be drastically
different, but speech-related gestures can cause crosscultural confusion
as well.

Speech-Independent Gestures

This category is for deliberate movements that can be specifically
defined by a word or a short phrase. They are true replacements for

speech and are used accordingly. Most speech-independent gestures have a common definition within the culture where they are used, and they generally take the form of a single gesture rather than multiple gestures put together.

Here are some examples of speech-independent gestures and their common meanings:

- Shoulder shrug—"I don't know" or "I don't care."
- Ring gesture (thumb and forefinger placed together to form a circle)—"good" or "okay" in the United States; "you're nothing" or "you're worthless" in France; "money" in Japan; and various vulgar sayings in Italy, Greece, and Turkey.
- Arm wave—"hello," "goodbye," or "I'm over here."
- Forefinger vertical to lips—"be quiet," or "stop talking."
- Arm straight in front, palm facing forward—"stop," or "stay back."
- Forefinger held up—"look up," "wait a moment," or "stop."
- Thumbs up—"yes," "good work," "I understand," or "let's go."

The range of gestures is tremendous, with many of them having different meanings and nuances based on context. The number of recognized speech-independent gestures varies in different parts of the world. For example, there are about 100 recognized gestures in the United States but over 250 recognized gestures in Israel.

Gesturing Expressiveness

Women are more expressive with their hands (for example, substituting gestures for words like okay) than are men.

Speech-Related Gestures

This category is for deliberate movements that accompany speech or
that are directly related to what is being said. They typically fall into
one of these general categories:

- Gestures related to what the speaker is talking about, whether
  the topic is abstract or concrete.

- Gestures indicating the speaker's relationship to or with the
  topic.

- Gestures used to punctuate or emphasize something the
  speaker says.

- Gestures used to regulate the flow of conversation between
  two or more people.

It's worth noting, however, that these are very loose categories
and that the gestures themselves can be difficult to place into the
appropriate category. Moreover, they vary from country to country
and culture to culture.

Overall meaning of a particular speech-related gesture may be
influenced by the size of the gesture (small hand movement vs. large
arm movement), the frequency of the gesture, and the context in
which it is used. Gestures are such an integral part of how we speak
that they show up even when we're speaking in a format where the
other person can't see us, such as on the telephone. Some people don't
even realize they do it. The next time you see someone talking on
the phone, pause for a moment and observe their gestures—you just
might be surprised at what you see!

Gestures influence your speech in a number of different ways. For
instance, if you are very passionate about the topic you're discussing,
then your gestures will probably be more frequent and more varied.
Or, if the topic is something you would typically do with your hands
(build a doghouse, wash a car, mow the lawn, etc.), you'll likely use

more gestures than if the topic is something you wouldn't typically do with your hands (history, current events, books, etc.).

Palms Up . . . A Surprisingly Consistent Cue

When people are communicating with you and standing fewer than six feet away, look at the position of their palms.

Are they typically open or up?

If so, that's rarely a bad sign. Usually this leads me to believe the person is being open, inviting, or at least vulnerable, curious, and interested.

On the other hand (wink), if you see palms down and away from you, that rarely signals comfort, vulnerability, or interest.

Touch

Touch is a unique element of body language because it carries with it such powerful connotations and so many different interpretations of intent. The four main categories of touch are:

- Professional—a personal trainer positioning you properly during an exercise, a dentist working on your teeth, a doctor examining you, a beautician cutting your hair.

- Social—a handshake, offering a hand to steady someone entering or exiting a vehicle, helping someone on or off with her coat.

- Friendship—a pat on the back, a touch of the arm, a hug, an arm around the shoulders.

- Intimacy—a kiss, a full embrace, holding hands, a touch of the cheek, rubbing the shoulders or the back.

The difficulty with touch as a nonverbal behavior is that different people have different definitions of which actions fall into which category. Their definitions may vary depending on age, gender, culture, circumstances, location, and the like, creating overlap between the different categories.

For instance, if your softball team wins a game and the team members hug each other to celebrate, those hugs have a different meaning than if they occurred during a business meeting, a walk in the park, or lunch in a restaurant. Gender differences abound as well. Women are generally more comfortable giving and receiving hugs or giving and receiving gentle touches with each other as a sign of friendship, while men are more comfortable using those same kinds of touch as signs of intimacy.

The purpose of touch is an important consideration as well. This is the area where most conflicts occur because the person performing the touch may have one purpose or intent, while the person receiving the touch may think it is based on a different purpose or intent. The meaning of touch can be very subjective, ranging across the following:

- Positive feedback
- Encouragement
- Support
- Negative feedback
- Anger
- Frustration
- Play
- Humor
- Influence
- Dominance
- Intimidation
- Stopping or starting an interaction
- Arousal
- Task completion

- Assistance

- Healing

- Symbolism

- Ritual

- Rank

- Status

The bottom line when it comes to touch is that it is one of the most subjective elements of body language. It is a good idea to take a conservative approach to using it in most situations and circumstances.

Touch, Power, and Nonverbals in the Office

Sexual harassment is a controversial issue 25 years after the institution of policies both ambiguous and rigid.

According to a recently published survey, "Gendered Constructions of Power During Discourse about Sexual Harassment: Negotiating Competing Meanings," published in *Sex Roles*, women interpret sexual harassment in terms of power. They tend to feel that every male at the office is a candidate for sexual harassment.

Men, however, believe that sexual harassment can only come from a superior (supervisor or manager).

The research indicates that women *are less likely* to experience touch from men as harassing if the man is attractive. And, if the man is very attractive, the touch is even less likely to be experienced as harassing.

For his unfortunate friends who are not so attractive, touching women can land them on the unemployment line. Women typically perceive touch from unattractive men as harassing.

In sum, women and men have very different views and behaviors related to sexual harassment, and, because of the distinctions, it appears that the problem isn't going away.

Posture

Most people think of posture as standing up straight, shoulders back, and eyes up. This is certainly one very broad way to describe posture, but there are smaller contributing aspects of posture as well. These include:

- Head position—tilted up, tilted down, tilted to the side.
- Shoulder position—forward, back, shrugged, tilted, slumped.
- Arm position—rigid, up, down, forward, straight, bent, crossed.
- Hips and legs—square and aligned, weight shifted to one side, one knee bent, hip thrust to either side, turned sideways, legs crossed.

The way you combine and use these various aspects changes the meaning and effectiveness of your message. For instance, if you are trying to make a good impression on a job interviewer or show interest in a one-on-one conversation, a common posture action is called mirroring. When you subtly mirror the posture of the other person you create a feeling of understanding, compatibility, and likeability. On the other hand, if you are trying to discourage a person's attention or end a conversation, your posture action might be just the opposite of mirroring. You may turn your back to the person, cross your arms in front of your chest, slump your shoulders, or lower your head and not make eye contact.

Posture has a big impact on first impressions, too. Picture yourself walking into a room for a business meeting. There are already two people seated at the meeting table—one is sitting upright with hands placed on the table, the other slumped back in the chair propping his or her face up with a hand on the chin. What is your initial impression of the first person? The second person?

Another interesting example of use of posture is in the sport of ballroom dancing. Couples assume a dance posture before they reach the dance floor, staying in that posture as they walk out and take their places before the music starts. When the music ends they stay in their dance posture until they have left the dance floor and are completely out of sight. Why do they do this? To impress the judges, of course. They don't want the judges to see them as anything other than polished, professional, and perfectly balanced.

Fast Fact

Some observers believe that head forward is a sign of being extroverted.

Not correct. There is no correlation.

Movement

Movement is an element of body language that many people do not fully appreciate in terms of its power and its flexibility. It can create a sense of interest and intimacy, a sense of power and domination, signal submission or retreat, and produce all kinds of emotional and physical reactions in other people.

Let's say you are walking in the shopping mall and you see someone moving toward you. If that person stays a certain distance away from you, his presence does not seem to be a threat; if, however, he moves too close to you, it's uncomfortable and you will either try to move away or face up to the perceived challenge of his movement. What is the magic distance for the change in perception of movement intent? That varies tremendously depending on the person, the culture, the context, and the environment.

If two people are having a disagreement and one person moves toward the other person, that movement will probably be intended and perceived as aggressive. If those same two people are having a conversation where emotions and feelings are being shared, that same movement will likely be intended and perceived as supporting or encouraging.

Movement can be used to generate familiarity with an audience. Think back to the last few presidential elections in the United States, specifically to the series of debates held between the two major candidates. The formal, structured debate is now joined by the more informal, town-hall style debate where the candidates are allowed to move around and approach the audience. This movement is very deliberate because it allows the candidate to connect better with the audience. Of course, some candidates are better at this than others, so naturally those who are good at it will push to use it in all of the debates, while those who are not good at it will push for the more structured format.

Appearance

This element of body language has to do with your physical appearance. It includes your body shape and size, your face and hair, your clothing, and the like. Whether we like it or not, appearance and physical attractiveness have a strong influence on how others receive and perceive our communication messages.

Some of the appearance factors to consider include:

- Body shape and size
- Facial shape
- Eyebrows
- Hair
- Height
- Color
- Cleanliness
- Clothing

- Accessories and jewelry
- Tattoos and body decoration
- Rough or smooth skin
- Manicured nails
- Makeup

Let's look at how some of these factors come into play.

Research studies have shown that a person of medium height with a muscular build is commonly perceived as mature and self-reliant while a person of medium height with a very thin, wiry build is commonly perceived as nervous and quieter. The modern profession of human resources administration focuses a lot of energy on teaching employers and interviewers how to control these natural tendencies and focus on the qualifications of the individual instead.

Let's go back to the example of walking into a meeting room where two people are already seated. One person is dressed neatly in a three-piece suit while the other person is dressed in jeans and a T-shirt. What first impression do you get now? What if the person wearing the suit has long hair and a bushy beard while the person wearing the jeans and T-shirt has a short, neat haircut and no facial hair? How does that affect or confuse your first impression.

Tattoos and body decoration have become extremely common, throwing a monkey wrench into the body language of appearance. Some of it is generational (the older you are the less likely you are to approve) and some of it is based in professional expectations (a banker vs. a bartender). Employers and parents often struggle with this issue, sometimes setting up huge conflicts and difficulties. Businesses have had to write specific policies into their dress codes while parents continue to fight the "my best friend has a pierced lip, why can't I have one?" battle.

In relationships of a personal nature, it's not a surprise that men are very much drawn to attractive women.

One of the keys to explaining a man's attraction to a woman is the waist-to-hip ratio. If a woman's waist-to-hip ratio is smaller than 24:36 for example, she will fit perfectly into a man's internal radar. If her waist-to-hip ratio is 1:1 or greater, in general, she will be filtered out by most men. They won't see her from the standpoint of sexuality and a love relationship.

Women also have an internal radar that filters men out, but it is more complex.

Women want a man to have waist-to-hip ratio of 1:1 or smaller. From an evolutionary perspective, fat men are obviously less likely to have great value to a woman, just as obese women are not likely to be of much value to men.

But there is more.

In the Japanese alphabet there is a character called Takai. (I think of George Takei from Start Trek to remember this.)

Takai is an adjective that refers to the "three Ts" that Japanese women look for in men. Those terms translate into English as:

- Tall
- High Income
- Intelligent

When women say they like men who are kind, that can typically be read as *in addition to* men who are tall, high income, and intelligent.

Later I'll show you how being deficient in one area can be made up for in another. In other words, just because a man isn't tall, doesn't mean he's automatically filtered out. He can make enough money to overcome his height disadvantage. He can be intelligent enough to overcome his height disadvantage. (The research shows money has more leverage than height.)

For now, simply realize that the research is simple.

Women who are attractive have numerous advantages in life *because* they are attractive. Men who are tall, intelligent, and wealthy have those same advantages.

Voice

The last element of body language I'll discuss is your voice. You might think of it as part of verbal language because it relates to words, but it's not. Voice is an important part of the nonverbal behaviors and cues that you both send and receive.

The common aspects of voice as body language include:

- Tone—warm, bored, enthusiastic, monotone, expressive.
- Pitch—high, low, ending words or phrase on an up or a down tone.
- Emphasis—less, more, rhythmic, unexpected, excessive, absent.
- Volume—loud, soft, projecting, variable, appropriate for the situation.
- Tempo—speed, variability, rhythm, pacing.
- Contrasts—loud, soft, fast, slow, high, low.
- Accent—nonnative speaker, pronunciations, specific emphasis.
- Emotion—sad, happy, excited, angry, afraid.
- Clarity—enunciation, mumbling, precision, distortion.
- Hesitation—starts and stops, struggling to find words.
- Pauses—for emphasis, for audience response, for dramatic effect.
- Language—slang, proper grammar, profanity, clichés, colloquialisms.

Let's say your voice is very soft, breathy, and high pitched. The first impression others have of you is likely to be that you are quiet, feminine, unsure of yourself, and young. If, however, your voice is very deep, loud, and robust, the first impression others have of you is likely to be that you are bold, knowledgeable, masculine, and mature.

Do you listen to the radio? Is there a DJ whose voice you recognize and know well? Whether you realize it or not, in your mind you have formed an impression of what that person looks like and perhaps even what his personality may be like. If you were to meet that person face to face, you would probably find the picture in your mind is quite different from reality.

When people's vocal aspects do not seem to match with their physical characteristics, it creates a conflict that may confuse or surprise others. A well-known example is Mike Tyson, a former professional boxer. At the height of his career he was the most dominant force in the sport of boxing, beating opponents with a ferocity and intensity that seemed almost unreal. His voice, however, was quite high pitched and sounded very feminine. His imposing, masculine body coupled with his small, feminine voice created a very conflicting impression of him indeed.

Some people will deliberately take on certain vocal aspects in an attempt to directly influence the nonverbal cues it creates. Women, for instance, may soften their tone and raise their pitch to convey intimacy. Both women and men may increase their volume and increase their tempo if they want to convey dominance, status, or persuasion.

Most people don't really know or understand the nonverbal influence of their voice. Compare this with actors, entertainers, newscasters, teachers, professional speakers, executives, and such. All of these people use their voices in specific ways to create specific impressions and nonverbal cues. The next time you watch the news, for example, close your eyes, and listen to the newscaster's voice. Listen to how his voice changes in tone, pitch, tempo, and the like, especially as he moves from serious news stories to lighter, human interest stories. You'll notice how his voice is used to set the tone for a story and convey the appropriate context.

Chapter 3 TAKEAWAYS

1. The elements of body language include both physical body parts and how those body parts are used.

2. The key elements include eyes, face, gestures, touch, posture, movement, appearance, and voice.

3. The eyes convey messages with both deliberate body language (eye contact, direction of gaze) and spontaneous body language (pupil dilation, blinking).

4. Facial expressions are thought by many to be the most important of all nonverbal behaviors. They convey emotion and regulate and direct an interaction.

5. Gestures are movements used to communicate a message or enhance communication of a message. They are deliberate and intentional; the two categories of gestures are speech-independent gestures (thumbs up, arm wave) and speech-related gestures (emphasize a point, describe a topic).

6. Touch generally falls into one of four categories: professional, social, friendship, and intimacy. There can be a tremendous amount of overlap between these categories due to factors such as age, gender, status, circumstances, and culture.

7. Posture includes several contributing aspects: head position, shoulder position, arm position, hips, and legs. It can be used in ways such as to influence first impressions, create understanding, and discourage attention.

8. Movement is powerful yet flexible in how it can be used. It can convey such things as familiarity, status, dominance, submission, aggression, support, and encouragement.

9. Appearance includes body shape and size, face and hair, clothing, and the like. It is particularly powerful when it comes to creating a first impression. There are some strong

generational differences in what is considered appropriate and inappropriate in terms of appearance.

10. Voice is a nonverbal tool that includes aspects such as tone, pitch, tempo, emphasis, emotion, and so on. Vocal aspects can be used deliberately to shape and influence nonverbal cues and how they are perceived by others.

Chapter 3 **WORKSHEET**

---

1. Review the Chapter 3 Takeaways and answer the following:
   - Which key point(s) did you find most interesting? Why?
   - Which key point(s) did you find most surprising? Why?

2. How do you use eye contact as part of your nonverbal behavior? Think of a time when you used it to show interest and attention. Describe what you did and the effect it had.

   Now think of a time when you used eye contact to show dominance or status. Describe what you did and the effect it had.

3. Videotape yourself giving a presentation or even participating in a conversation. Go back and look at the tape, noting your body language and what it conveyed.

4. Use a tape recorder to record your voice as you have a normal conversation. Play it back and listen to the nonverbal cues it conveys. What would you like to change? How can you achieve it?

4 | Context and Environment

The meaning and interpretation of body language is greatly affected by the context and environment in which it takes place.

Some nonverbal behavior is appropriate in some situations but not in others; some has an entirely different meaning in some situations compared with others. In this chapter I'll explore these concepts in more detail so by the end you'll have a better understanding of how context and environment influence body language, both in terms of appropriateness and meaning.

How Context and Environment Influence Body Language

Context and environment influence body language in ways both obvious and subtle. Some are due to social norms, some are due to life experience, and some are due to individual personality and self-esteem. There are generational differences, gender differences, and cultural differences, as well.

It really all comes down to perceptions. How do you perceive the context and environment where you are right now? If you're at home you're probably dressed casually, maybe drinking a soda or a cup of coffee, and there might be music, TV, or other people making noise in the background. You may or may not be taking notes as you read, and if you are, it's probably notes in the margin of the book.

If you're in the office, however, you're probably dressed in business clothes, sitting at a desk or meeting room table, and hearing the typical background noises of the office environment. You may even have a file folder set aside where you keep copies of your worksheets, takeaways, and any notes you've taken while reading.

Why the differences? It has to do in part with your perceptions of the context and environment in which you're operating. Some of the common categories of perceptions include:

- Formality
- Privacy
- Familiarity
- Warmth
- Distance
- Constraint
- Time
- Other people
- Physical environment

How you perceive each of these things (and how others around you perceive each of these things) is a driving force behind the appropriateness and meaning of your body language.

Formality

The perception of formality or informality is one that can vary greatly depending on your life experiences and social environment. The people, the activity, the physical objects, and social expectations all influence your perception of formality. For instance, your weekly staff meeting may have a certain level of formality, but what happens when the division manager or member of the executive team is scheduled to attend? The meeting takes on a higher level of formality because of the higher status of a person who will attend.

Restaurants are another great example of how perceptions of formality and informality are created. What do you find in a typical fast-food place? Self-service, tables and chairs attached to the floor, paper napkins, and a central area for condiments and drinks. All of these things create an informal atmosphere that is accepted and understood. Now, what do you find in a higher end restaurant? Hostess seating, tablecloths, wait staff to serve you, and everything you need brought right to your table. These things contribute to a more formal atmosphere that, again, is accepted and understood.

So what is the effect of all this on body language and nonverbal communication? In general, the more formality you perceive the less relaxed your body language will be. Your nonverbal behaviors will be more conservative and controlled to fit in with accepted expectations for the understood level of formality. You may feel hesitant about showing your true thoughts during a conversation, so you make a deliberate effort to keep your facial expression and posture neutral.

Privacy

The perception of privacy is an indicator of how likely you think it is you'll be overheard or seen by someone else. It is influenced by the size of the space where you are, whether it is fully enclosed, how many other people are nearby, and how easy it is for others to see you in that space.

For example, when you go to see your doctor the examination room is fully enclosed and access to the room is limited. The perception is one of great privacy. The same is true of being in an office with a door, your home, and the like. Your visibility to others is also an important factor in the perception of privacy. Imagine carrying on a heated discussion in a room with glass walls where everyone outside can see inside. How does it feel? Now imagine the same discussion in a room with no windows and the door closed. Any difference? I imagine so.

The perception of privacy affects how intimately you will interact with others. In general, the more privacy you perceive the more comfortable you will feel sharing personal messages, thoughts, and information. You will tend to sit closer to the other person(s) and lean in. The greater the privacy the safer it feels for you to let go and allow your body language to reflect what's truly on your mind.

Beware of This Myth

For years we've thought that when a woman leans forward into a conversation with someone it is a sign of significant interest and attraction.

However, this has not proven to be true in the majority of situations.

However, when men lean into a conversation (toward a counterpart) that typically does indicate a greater degree of interest or trust than existed previously.

Familiarity

The perception of familiarity affects how you interact with people and the environment and is based on how new or different you perceive a situation to be. For example, when you meet a new person you automatically go into a more formal, conservative body language mode. You don't know the person yet so your nonverbal behavior signals something along the lines of, "I need to learn more about you before I can relax."

Think about the first time you drove a car, started a new job, tried a new sport, or the like. Your perception of familiarity was likely very low so your body language reflected a great deal of caution and deliberation. Now think about those same things after you had done them for a few weeks. Your perception of familiarity had grown so your nonverbal behaviors reflected less caution and more comfort.

Retail stores know all about the perception of familiarity and make deliberate attempts to influence yours. Large chain stores such as Target, Wal-Mart, Shopko, an so on, typically build almost all of their stores with the same or similar floor plan. Why? So no matter where you go, when you walk into one of their stores you will find it familiar and comfortable. This helps entice you to make more purchases.

The perception of familiarity affects how openly and honestly you will interact with others. In general, the more familiarity you perceive, the more willing you are to allow your body language to relax. You walk more confidently, your tone of voice is calmer and stronger, and you can do whatever you came to do without exploring the environment first.

Warmth

The perception of warmth is based on psychological factors rather than physical comfort factors. The warmth of a particular place or area is affected by colors, textures, physical objects, and the like. For instance, walking into the hardware store you perceive much less warmth than you do walking into a furniture store. The furniture store uses softer colors, displays wonderfully textured items, and is filled with a sense of comfort.

Here's another example. Think about your local espresso coffee shop and the decor inside. It probably features muted colors and a collection of chairs and sofas, all of which create a greater perception of warmth. And that greater warmth is what entices you to stay a little longer, linger a bit, and spend more money.

The perception of warmth is closely related to familiarity, but you do not always have to be familiar with an environment to perceive its warmth. That warmth will encourage you to show more relaxed body language, such as an open body position when sitting or standing, conversations held while standing or sitting closer together, and generally relaxed nonverbal behaviors.

Distance

The perception of distance is based on both physical distances and psychological distances. It is possible for you to feel physically close and psychologically distant at the same time, and the reverse is true as well.

For instance, let's say you are riding on a crowded transit bus, surrounded by people you don't know. The physical distances are rather close but psychologically you feel distant because you are among strangers. You can't make changes to the physical circumstances, but you can make changes to your body language as a way to deal with the psychological circumstances. You might choose to make as little eye contact as possible, remain very still, and stay silent. Sometimes, though, the opposite happens and you might laugh nervously, comment to the people around you about the close quarters, and the like.

The perception of distance affects how you interpret a situation and the kinds of nonverbal behaviors you exhibit. When physical and psychological distances are perceived as equal to each other your body language will typically match appropriately: relaxed and open when distance is small, reserved and more formal when distance is large. When the two aspects are in conflict, however—such as in the transit bus example—your resulting body language may be somewhat conflicting or unpredictable as well.

Want to Send a Strong Rapport-Building Message with Proxemics?

When you walk near someone else's space, pause and stay out of it. Initiate your conversation and then about 30 seconds into the conversation, open your palm to the chair in front of you.

"May I?"

You've now been authorized into their space.

Typically, the person doesn't feel comfortable at this point. Stay with your back in the chair.

Talk about something that does not require the privacy of a really soft spoken voice.

Then when you are going to communicate something that is of greater concern, lean forward a bit in the chair.

This will show respect, appreciation, and liking for your counterpart.

Constraint

The perception of constraint relates to how you perceive your ability to leave a particular situation. The more constrained you feel, the more out of control you feel, and the more reserved your body language will be. For instance, let's say you are attending a workshop or seminar required by your employer. Regardless of the size of the room you are in, you will feel constrained in that situation because you know you are not free to leave.

Contrast that with what happens when you walk into a restaurant. If it is crowded and the wait time is very long, you don't have to stay there. You can leave and go somewhere else. Your body language will tend to be more relaxed and comfortable because you feel free to make your own choice, not have your choice made for you.

The perception of constraint can vary in its severity and duration. Let's say you're a college student who lives in the dorm. Spring break comes along and it's time to go back home for a week. Chances are you perceive (accurately, most likely) greater constraints in that environment than you do back at school. Because it's only for a week, though, you (and your parents) just deal with it. What happens, though, when it's summer break and you move back home for two or three months? The perceived restraints might not be so tolerable for that length of time, and, if not addressed, your body language and nonverbal behaviors will quickly start to reveal your true inner feeling.

Time

The perception of time can take many different forms. You might be up against a tight deadline, and the perception of a short time frame leads to tense body language and nonverbal behaviors. Or, you might be scheduled to meet someone at a specific time but that person is late, so your body language might reflect irritation or even lack of respect for someone who can't get places on time.

Let's say you are driving somewhere with a group of people you don't know very well. Even if you'll only be in the car together for an hour or so, you might perceive that length of time as quite negative. Your nonverbal behaviors are likely to be reserved, especially given the close quarters and lack of familiarity with the other people. What would happen to your perception if, once the drive got under way, you found you really like the other people, and there is a strong connection among you? Chances are the time spent in the car will suddenly not seem so negative and may even seem to pass by more quickly.

The perception of time influences body language in terms of how you approach lengths of time as well as how you interpret others' use of time. Culture plays a strong role in time perceptions as well. In the United States, people are driven to be on time and pack as much into every day as possible. In Brazil, however, time is viewed more as a guideline than a hard-and-fast rule. The more relaxed approach to time is reflected in Brazilians' more relaxed body language and nonverbal behaviors.

Other People

The perception of other people is related to the perceptions of privacy and familiarity. When other people are around, you automatically make a judgment about how active or passive those people are in the environment.

Are those other people active participants in the conversation? Are they close enough to overhear the conversation? If you perceive others as actively involved then your body language will adapt accordingly. You may make eye contact with more people, address your message to more people, and generally practice more conservative body language.

If, however, you perceive others as not actively involved, then your body language will reflect that as well. You might turn your back to others, avoid eye contact, or simply not include them in the conversation. However, your perception of other people is not necessarily related to their physical distance from you. Think about the last time you were riding in a cab. The driver is physically very close but you may perceive that person as a passive participant and avoid eye contact, sit in silence, or otherwise send the nonverbal message that you don't wish to interact.

The perception of other people affects body language by creating situations where you might be more reserved or formal if you do not know the others. If you know the other people well, though, your nonverbal behaviors will reflect that familiarity and level of comfort.

Physical Environment

The perception of physical environment is related to the perception of warmth, privacy, and distance. It is different, though, in that this perception is strongly affected by physical placement of items, lighting, sounds, and even building architecture. These factors (and others) interact to influence your perception of the physical environment around you.

For instance, if you walk into a room where the furniture is laid out in rows, all facing the same direction, your nonverbal behaviors will likely become more formal and reserved because the environment is more formal and structured. If, however, you walk into a room where the furniture is arranged in small clusters with comfortable chairs, your nonverbal behaviors will likely relax because the environment is more intimate and personal.

Building architecture has a lot to do with perceptions of physical environment as well. When a building is designed with communal areas, wide hallways, and traffic flow that brings people together, the physical environment may be large but still perceived as friendly and comfortable. Modern architectural design considers these issues; to see for yourself, take a walk through an older building and a walk through a newer building. You will likely notice many differences and your perceptions will likely be different as well.

Same Body Language, Different Perceptions

Depending on the context and environment, the same body language can have vastly different meanings. This may occur if you are in an unfamiliar environment where you don't know the expectations or it can occur if the people around you view the situation in a different context than you do. Cultural differences, gender differences, and age differences can affect perceptions of body language as well.

For instance, a man who speaks forcefully and uses a strong, upright body posture is often perceived as being capable, worthy, and strong in a business environment. A woman who does those same things, though, is often perceived as pushy, aggressive, and not very likable. Now put both the man and woman behaving that way in a military environment and they will probably both be perceived as capable and effective.

Here's another example. You're in a classroom teaching a group of students when you notice one of them sitting with his arms crossed, back slumped, and looking bored. Your perception is that he is not paying attention to what you are teaching. Later that day you walk past the lounge area of the student union building and see the same student in the same position. Your perception this time around is quite different—he looks tired, unhappy, and perhaps frustrated about something. You saw the same body language in a different context and environment and experienced very different perceptions.

Sometimes, however, the differences in context or environment are not quite as clear or easily identified. Take eye blinking, for example. Rapid blinking is generally perceived as a sign of nervousness or even deceit in nearly every context where there is not an obvious physical reason for that nonverbal behavior. But what if there is a not-so-obvious reason for it? For instance, some medications cause side effects that include rapid blinking of the eyes. This is not the kind of thing you would automatically find out about a person right away, and it is not something that would be immediately obvious.

When Body Language and Context Are in Conflict

When body language and context are in conflict, most people default to placing more value on body language. Why? Because in general, body language and nonverbal behaviors are much harder to fake than are words or speech. Your words may say one thing, but if your body language says something different then the people around you will tend to believe your body language more than your words.

It's important to note, though, that not all people default to the nonverbal behaviors when messages are in conflict. They might not be as attuned to body language in general or they may have a positive pre-conceived opinion about the person delivering the conflicted messages. In the latter case, the positive opinion will tend to outweigh the negatives of a conflicting message, at least for a little while.

If your body language is not perceived as appropriate or normal for the context in which it takes place, others will tend toward three basic steps in an attempt to understand and resolve the conflict:

1. They feel confused and uncertain about you and what is happening.

2. They will try to figure out what is going on by looking for other information and clues that might explain the apparent conflict.

3. If they can't find the information they need to explain the conflict then they will likely have a negative reaction to you.

Sometimes, though, body language and context are deliberately in conflict. A discussion about irony or an attempt at sarcasm nearly always includes some type of body language (movement, tone of voice, etc.) that conflicts with the context and the specific situation.

The bottom line here is that conflicts between context and body language are inevitable and there is no clear, certain way to determine how those conflicts will be perceived and resolved by others. If you are the sender then it is in your best interest to reduce the perceived conflict as much as possible, and if you are the receiver then it is in your best interest to make every effort to resolve the perceived conflict without resorting to speculation or unsupported opinions.

The Context ... A Simple Analysis

Where did your business counterpart take you to lunch? Mc-Donald's?

That probably signals the value of your business to him or the value of *you* to him.

(Nothing wrong with McDonald's. I like McDonald's, just not for business meetings.)

Did your client or counterpart take you to an elegant restaurant?

That also probably signals the value of your business and/or you, to him.

You want to look at this as a good sign.

You also want to consider it from a strategic point.

If I were to induce reciprocity instead of letting it occur naturally, I'd probably take you out to an expensive restaurant.

Key Point: Reading People Starts with the Context

Being able to read people is much more than simply noticing gestures and translating those gestures into words. Understanding what they are really saying to you, is much more than just the words and body language.

In fact, translating nonverbal communication (body language, the context, use of space, symbols, dress, and time), is far more about the secret language of influence that we all use every day.

Unfortunately, there are not many universal standards in the hidden language.

The first factor I look at when consciously analyzing anyone's communication or body language is the context.

Nothing matters more.

Is the person whose mind you wish to read (essentially what people ask me to do when reading nonverbal communication) in:

A church?

A synagogue?

A mosque?

An elementary school?

A prison?

A television studio?

An elegant restaurant?

A lounge in Vegas?

A hotel lobby?

At the beach?

A grocery store?

An automotive dealership?

where (handwritten)

That's the *frame* of the context.

The next factor in the context is the event—the why—of why the person is there.

Because they have to be?

Because they are holding the party?

Because they were invited?

Because they are working there?

Because they are visiting?

Because they are scouting for a partner (long- or short-term)?

Because they are attempting to relax?

why (handwritten)

That's the second and smaller frame.

That means that generally the smaller frame is not as all-encompassing as the large frame.

You could be at a birthday party in a church and you are going to behave not in accordance with the birthday party but within the rules governing the church.

Make sense?

So, you have "where" and "why" and they are both crucial frames.

Those two frames tell you a lot about the person right there.

For whatever reason the person is at the location, it *is* for a reason.

They may wish they were somewhere else, but for the most part it was their choice to be at this location.

And, it also tells you what the person is not doing.

For example, if the person is at home with her husband on a Friday night, she's not out at a bar with her girlfriends—for some reason. We don't know why, but we do know the facts.

Those facts matter a great deal in reading people.

Have you ever been somewhere you didn't want to be?

Can I give you a list?!

So we all understand that we may not want to be at this location and event but we have agreed to be there.

In all probability the more uncomfortable they are in the situation, the more "leakage" they will express.

In other words, they will unwittingly send more unconscious cues and clues as to why they are in a situation when they really don't want to be there. They don't consciously reveal this information through their body language or any of the other nonverbal communication channels.

But they do . . . and they are clueless.

Most people will never pick up on these clues.

If you ever hear me say, "The context is everything," I'm not being literal, but never analyze anything, never be influenced without considering the context first. It's the biggest part of the Secret Language of Business.

Chapter 4 **TAKEAWAYS**

1. Context and environment are important to the meaning and interpretation of body language. Their influence can be both obvious and subtle.

2. Conflict occurs when there are differences in social norms, life experience, personality, self-esteem, age, gender, culture, and the like.

3. The key perceptions of context and environment include formality, privacy, familiarity, warmth, distance, constraint, time, other people, and physical environment.

4. The same body language can produce very different perceptions depending on context and environment.

5. Conflicts are likely to occur when you are in unfamiliar places, with unfamiliar people, or simply don't have an awareness of the social norms and expectations of that particular context.

6. When body language and context are in conflict, most of the time body language will be perceived as more reliable but this is not a hard-and-fast rule. Many things can affect this judgment, such as prior positive view of the person, obvious sarcasm or irony, and often just a lack of attention and awareness of nonverbal behaviors and cues.

Chapter 4 **WORKSHEET**

---

1. Review the Chapter 4 Takeaways and answer the following:
   - Which key point(s) did you find most interesting? Why?
   - Which key point(s) did you find most surprising? Why?

2. Look around the environment where you are right now. What are your perceptions of the following:

Formality

Privacy

Familiarity

Warmth

Distance

Constraint

Time

Other people

Physical environment

How do your perceptions of these categories influence your current body language?

5

Proxemics: The Secret Language of Business . . . Up Close

You've probably had this experience at some point in your life. Someone walks up to talk with you and stands so close you feel uncomfortable and maybe even subconsciously take a step backwards. Or, someone sits down next to you so close that you squirm a bit and slide away. What has happened? Someone else has invaded your personal space, and that creates a strong reaction inside of you.

What Is Proxemics?

The study of personal space and how humans use distance in general is called proxemics. The term "proxemics" was first used in 1963 by an anthropologist and researcher named E.T. Hall, who was fascinated with how people communicate nonverbally using spatial relationships and territory. Through his research he demonstrated and defined four areas of space relevant to proxemics:

1. Intimate space
2. Personal space

3. Social space

4. Public space

There is no single set distance for each of these spaces because there is so much variation. The use of space is a dynamic process; it shifts and adjusts depending on personalities, situations, social perceptions, cultures, and more.

Very few factors matter as much in the secret language of business as proxemics.

Research and study, though, have identified a general range of distances for each of these spaces and the types of interactions that occur in each one. As I define each one in more detail, think of them as concentric circles with you standing in the middle and the circles radiating outward.

Intimate Space

This area extends from your body out to around 18 inches or so. As the name implies, only those with whom you have the most intimate relationships can move into this space without you moving away. It is the range of space typically used for intimate touch, whispers, hugs, kisses, and the like.

Personal Space

This area starts at about 18 inches away from you and extends out to about four feet or so. It is the area reserved for interactions with good friends and people with whom you have a solid personal connection. Some body language experts refer to this as your "personal bubble" or just your bubble. Interestingly, this is the space most likely to fluctuate from culture to culture.

Social Space

This area starts about four feet away from you and extends out to about 12 feet or so. It is the area reserved for interactions with new acquaintances, casual acquaintances, and anybody with whom you don't have a high comfort level.

Public Space

This final area starts about 12 feet away from you and extends out to about 25 feet or beyond. It is the area of interaction among the general public, whether it's walking past each other in a park, speaking to an audience, or walking through the mall.

I mentioned earlier about cultural differences in proxemics and space, especially when it comes to personal space. The differences among cultures are marked, and when they are not understood, acknowledged, and respected it can quickly lead to a great deal of misunderstanding and trouble.

For instance, in northern European countries such as Great Britain, Norway, and Sweden, personal space is generally quite large. In those countries you would not stand as close to someone, and you certainly wouldn't touch someone unless you were very good or intimate friends. This all seems very normal to people who live in those cultures, but it would seem exceedingly strange to people from other cultures.

If you were interacting with someone from Italy, Spain, the Middle East, or a Latin American country you would find the personal space distance to be extremely small. It is not unusual for people from these areas to feel perfectly comfortable in very close proximity to each other, sometimes even face to face. Touch is an accepted practice in these cultures, even among new acquaintances.

You can imagine, then, the potential for misunderstandings when these cultures intersect. Those with a need for a larger personal space may be seen as cold, distant, reserved, or unemotional, while those comfortable with a smaller personal space may be seen as rude, inappropriate, or much too forward.

The Relationship between Body Language and Proxemics

The relationship between body language and proxemics is complex and not fully understood, but it is also extremely revealing and interesting. So much of proxemics is based on personal preference and social perceptions that body language and nonverbal behaviors become even more critical to observe and understand.

Body language is the primary tool you use to communicate with others about your own specific distances for each category of space. This allows you to avoid verbal messages that may be awkward to send or even considered rude by some people. Rather, nonverbal behaviors are a subtle means of sending and receiving messages that help negotiate the use of space and territory around you.

Giving Space for Men and Women

Men stand and sit further away from others for comfort.

Women stand and sit closer for comfort.

Women sit further away from men for comfort.

Another advantage of using body language rather than words is its dynamic and flexible nature. This is important because as a conversation proceeds you may feel varying levels of comfort with the other person and nonverbal behaviors allow you to communicate those varying levels in real time. As you become more comfortable with another person, your body language indicates it's okay to move closer into your spaces, but if at any point you feel less comfortable or discover something you perceive to be negative about that other person you can just as easily indicate the need for more distance.

The classic illustration of body language and proxemics at work is the first date. If you were to observe two people on a first date you would see the ebb and flow of nonverbal behaviors throughout the interaction. For instance, they might start by shaking hands and sit down on opposite sides of the table. As they get to know each other and feel more comfortable with each other, you would see them leaning toward each other more, perhaps sliding their chairs closer together, and occasionally reaching out to touch the other person's hand quickly and lightly.

Another good illustration is to watch people walking on any city sidewalk. If the sidewalk is not crowded you will see individuals casually and subtly moving to maximize the distance between themselves and others on the sidewalk, particularly those walking toward them. As the sidewalk becomes more crowded, however, it becomes more difficult to maintain those spaces so new nonverbal behaviors will emerge. People will turn away from each other slightly as they pass, sending the message that the spacing is too close for total comfort.

Proxemics and body language also have practical applications in the workplace. For instance, if you are working with someone else on a project and the two of you sit down to discuss it you'll likely sit with an adjoining corner between you if your focus is going to be on the table in front of you. This position allows both of you to easily see the materials before you and to keep your attention on those materials instead of directly on each other.

Reading Men and Women when Seated

Women orient their heads and bodies toward conversation partners more than men.

When women are with someone they know, they prefer to sit side by side; men prefer face to face.

When with someone they don't know, the opposite is true.

If your discussion with someone else is more adversarial, difficult, or simply a getting-to-know-you type of conversation, you'll most likely sit on opposite sides of the table, facing each other. From this position you can most directly observe and interpret body language, maintain eye contact, and use the table as a safe buffer zone between you.

How Big Is Your Bubble?

So how big is your bubble? You may never have thought about it (most people don't) because it is just an automatic part of who you are, but if you take the time to understand your own preferences you can better understand the kinds of nonverbal messages you send to other people.

For instance, if you have a large personal space and your supervisor or manager has a smaller personal space interactions between the two of you may not be so smooth. When you're talking with each other your supervisor probably stands closer to you than you would like, causing your body language to send "step back" or "get away from me" messages, which, in turn, may be perceived by your supervisor as cold, rude, or disrespectful. Not exactly a great pattern of communication in terms of your work and career.

What can you do about it? Increase your awareness, first of all. Before you can consciously adapt your nonverbal behaviors you have to be aware of what they are and how they are triggered at various points of your space boundaries. Using the example above, if you know your supervisor tends to move in closer than you might like, you can choose to either say something to him or her, or adapt your own responses when the two of you interact. You might make a point of sitting on the opposite side of the meeting room table, for example, or keeping a desk or office chair between you when you talk. I can't tell you which idea is the best, though; you need to consider the advantages and disadvantages of both approaches and decide for yourself the best course of action.

Different Environments, Different Distances

You also have different space distances in different environments. The workplace, public places, your home, the gym, the shopping mall—your boundaries will shift a bit in all of these environments. Even if you interact with the exact same people in two different places, your space distances will likely change from one place to another.

An excellent example of this is the office party. In the workplace you have specific boundaries that are appropriate for the business nature of the environment and status relationships among you and your coworkers. Now put all of you together in a social environment such as an office party, and just see how subtly your boundaries change. Your conversations will likely be lighter and not work related, so you may feel more comfortable when coworkers stand a little closer for friendly exchanges.

Gender differences are also quite pronounced when it comes to proxemics. In general, women are much more comfortable with a small personal space when interacting with other women, regardless of the environment. Change that interaction to a man and a woman, though, and the environment makes a huge difference. A larger personal space is more typical in the workplace, while a closer personal space is more typical in a social situation. When it comes to men interacting with other men, larger spaces are generally the norm.

Using Proxemics to Improve Your Communications

You can use proxemics to improve your communications, both as the sender and the receiver. I talked about this with you as the sender in the previous section on your bubble, so I won't repeat that information here. The most important point for you to remember is to be aware of the nonverbal messages you're sending and modify them if possible and if appropriate.

When you are the message receiver there is a great deal you can do with the nonverbal information you take in via proxemics. It can help you gauge how a business meeting is proceeding, what's going on with a negotiation, if your date is enjoying your company, and how your new office partner feels about the division of space between your desks.

Proxemics is also an invaluable tool if you interact with someone from another culture, no matter the environment. Learn a little bit about what to expect if you plan to travel to Spain, for example, or Great Britain. This will help you better understand and receive messages from the people you meet and help you determine the best ways to send your own messages while there. In business, it is critical to know about cultural differences to avoid misunderstandings, difficult negotiations, or even losing a valued customer.

Overall, proxemics is one of the most interesting areas of body language and nonverbal behaviors. I strongly encourage you to become aware of people's space as they approach you, and how they respond to you as you approach them.

How do they shift their bodies?

What do their eyes do?

Where do their hands go from and to?

Chapter 5 TAKEAWAYS

1. Proxemics is the study of personal space and how humans use distance in communication and interpersonal interactions.

2. There are four spaces relevant to proxemics:

    Intimate space. From your body out to about 18 inches.

    Personal space. From 18 inches out to about four feet.

Social space. From four feet out to about 12 feet.

Public space. From 12 feet out to about 25 feet or beyond.

3. The relative size of these spaces varies from person to person, from environment to environment, and from culture to culture.

4. You should work to become aware of your own space distances to maximize your own ability to adapt and adjust to different situations.

5. You can use proxemics to better understand your interactions with others, both as the sender and as the receiver.

Chapter 5 WORKSHEET

---

1. Review the Chapter 5 Takeaways and answer the following:
   - Which key point(s) did you find most interesting? Why?
   - Which key point(s) did you find most surprising? Why?

2. Think about your own space distances—intimate, personal, social, and public. For each category, write down at least one example of when you have had an interaction where that space was violated or infringed upon.

   Intimate:

   Personal:

   Social:

   Public:

3. For one whole day, focus on observing space distances and interactions among other people. Make notes about what you see in places such as the mall, the office, a business meeting, a restaurant, or wherever else you go.

6 | What Does Your Body Language Say about You?

Your body language is constantly communicating messages about you, messages that relate to your thoughts, feelings, emotions, attitudes, self confidence, and more. But what exactly are those messages? What nonverbal information are you sending, and how is the information received and interpreted by others?

In this chapter I'll focus on six main categories of what your body language communicates about you:

1. Status

2. Dominance

3. Submission

4. Uncertainty

5. Confidence

6. Personal identity

These categories each describe an overall impression others might form about you based on your nonverbal cues. You will probably recognize something about yourself in each section because everybody cycles through these categories to one degree or another. As you read through the details of each one, take some mental notes about situations where you think you might come across in that particular way. Is it a common occurrence? Is it something you have to consciously choose? Is it something that just seems to happen before you know it?

Once you have greater awareness of what your body language says about you in a variety of circumstances you can begin making deliberate choices about when, where, and how to use different nonverbal behaviors. Think about which behaviors serve you well and choose how to use them more often. Think also about which behaviors are not serving you so well or are even holding you back from your goals, then choose how to change or use them less often.

Are you ready? Let's get going and see where it all leads.

Status

Human beings communicate status through a variety of actions. The first and arguably most important is increasing height to convey a higher status. Of course you can't simply will yourself to grow taller, but you can carry yourself and position yourself in ways that make you appear taller. Other nonverbal cues of status include touch and location.

Posture. This is the foundation of the appearance of height. When you hold yourself with back straight, shoulders back, and head up, your body becomes taller, in some cases as much as a couple of inches or more. You can measure this for yourself with the help of a wall, a pencil, a ruler, and a helper. Stand with your back to the wall, allowing yourself to slump over, slouch your shoulders forward, and lower your head. Ask your helper to place a pencil mark on the wall to show your height. Now repeat the process, but this time stand up straight with your shoulders back and your head up. Look at the difference between the two marks and you'll see concrete proof of how much posture affects height.

But wait a minute. What about people who are just plain shorter than most everyone else? Their posture won't increase their height a huge amount, so does this mean they are destined to always have a lower status? The answer is no. Even an extremely short person can convey a higher status with a combination of good posture and other nonverbal cues I'll discuss a bit later. He may have to work at it a bit harder to overcome stereotyping by other people, but there is no reason a person of small stature cannot convey status using good posture.

Touch. Most body language experts agree that touch can be used and interpreted as a sign of status. In general, the person with the higher status will initiate touch, whether it's shaking hands, a pat on the back, or a hand on the arm. What's more, when other people observe an interaction like this, they perceive the initiator as having higher status. Think about this for a moment. When you look around a room full of people you'll likely see many different interactions occurring all at once, and you start to form perceptions about the relative status of the people participating in those interactions.

That man you see circulating around the room, shaking hands and patting others on the back? He appears to be someone important or of higher status. Or what about the woman who walks up to that man and reaches out to shake hands? By initiating touch she is conveying to him and to the rest of the world that she views her status as at least equal to and possibly even greater than his.

Location. What happens when a group of people walk into a room and sit down at a table? The person with the highest status will generally choose a seat at the head of the table while the others find seats further down along the sides of the table. The head location is perceived and accepted as being reserved for the person of highest status.

The concept of seating location as a sign of status occurs in many different circumstances. At a concert, the best and most expensive seats are right up front. In a parking lot, the CEO's reserved space is located right next to the building instead of down past a long line of other cars. In royal circles, both modern and historic, the monarch sits at the head of the table or the front of the room, with other people seated or lined up at varying distances. The closer a person is located to the monarch, the higher that person's status.

Children are especially attuned to the status that goes with physical location. When grandparents come to visit they may jostle with each other a bit for the privilege of sitting next to Grandma or Grandpa. The child who sits closest wins and achieves a higher status. Of course, Grandma and Grandpa understand the importance of status, and that's why they make sure each child gets a turn to sit closest and feel that sense of privilege and status.

Dominance

Dominance is closely related to status, and in some circumstances they are practically interchangeable, but there is a slightly different nuance to dominance that I think is worth exploring. Status is generally used to describe differences in title, heritage, or perceived hierarchy in a larger context, often related to groups. Dominance, on the other hand, is generally used to describe relative power and control within specific interactions or relationships. It is demonstrated in a number of ways, most of which involve some difference in relative position. I'm going to focus on relative position in terms of elevation, hand position, and body movement.

Elevation. I use the word elevation to describe the relative physical position of two people when one person is higher than the other. The higher you are compared with someone else, the more dominant you appear. For instance, when you go to a conference or presentation, the speaking platform is almost always raised or elevated above the floor level. Why? It allows the audience to see the speaker more easily, of course, but it also puts the speaker in a dominant position. He is in charge, in control, and perceived as important.

Dominance in a relationship might show up as a conversation with one person sitting and one person standing, or sitting on a couch watching TV with one person sitting upright and the other slouched down and leaning on the first person. In a casual interaction, dominance might appear as one person perching on the edge of a table while the other person is seated, or one person standing on the high side of an incline and the other standing on the low side, rather than the two of them standing side by side.

The relationship between elevation and dominance appears throughout our media culture as well. The dashing hero of a movie is almost always portrayed as taller than the other characters, giving him an elevated position. Sometimes this requires clever camera angles or set adjustments to boost one person higher or move another person down lower, all to create the appearance of a difference in elevation and therefore a sense of dominance.

Here's another example. The next time you watch a news program where several panelists are sitting arrayed around a large desk or table, take note of how little difference there is between the height of people in the group. Chances are that the producers have done some adjusting to the height of chairs to create the illusion that all are equal and nobody is dominant.

Hand position. The relative position of hands is another indicator of dominance. In ancient times when two rivals met face to face they would posture and push during the greeting, each attempting to end up with his hands in a higher position than the other person. The person with the upper hand was perceived as dominant, and the phrase "have the upper hand" can be traced directly back to this pattern.

Palm position is important, too, as the person whose hand is positioned palm down is perceived as more dominant than the person whose hand is positioned palm up. Observe closely the next time you see two people shake hands; the person whose hand is extended with the palm facing more downward is sending a message of dominance over the person whose hand is extended with the palm facing more upward.

The dominance of hand position even shows up when two people are walking together and holding hands. The dominant person will clasp the other's hand with palm facing backward and slightly on top; the other person will clasp hands palm facing forward and slightly on the bottom. For instance, a parent holds a child's hand when crossing the street, and guess whose hand is in the upper position? The parent's, of course.

Body movement. Dominance is also expressed through general body movement. Moving toward another person or stepping in front of another person can both be perceived as dominant behaviors. Why? Because the dominant person is moving into a relative position that is higher, closer, in front of, or otherwise stronger than the other person's.

Here's an example from the real world. In an elementary school classroom, kids usually line up to go just about anywhere. They line up to go to lunch, out to recess, to the library, and so on. The front of the line is most desirable because it is dominant, so you will see kids actively maneuvering their bodies to get as close to the front as possible. That's one reason why teachers select a daily or weekly line leader to avoid conflict over who gets to be all the way in front and to give every child an opportunity to take the lead in the dominant position.

Another example can be seen when two people are arguing with each other. If the argument becomes heated you'll likely see one or both of them making body movements forward and toward each other rather than backward and away from each other. Controlling distance and controlling movement are both behaviors that show dominance, so when two people are both vying for that control and end up bumping up against each other the situation often escalates even further because neither one is willing to back down.

Submission

At the opposite end of the spectrum from dominance is submission, or body language that sends the message you perceive and/or allow the other person to have control. In the animal kingdom you can see all sorts of submissive behaviors, from the wolf that rolls over and exposes his belly to show submission to the pack leader to the wild stallion that turns and runs when a more powerful stallion takes over the herd of mares.

In the human world, the same types of behaviors are used to signal submission. Lowering the body, averting the eyes, and moving away are all powerful, nonverbal cues that send a submissive message.

Body lowering. When a person uses a body lowering behavior, it places that person in a lower relative position to another person. And because elevation indicates dominance, making a conscious choice to take a lower position sends a message of willingness to submit to the dominance of another person.

For example, in Japan it is a traditional greeting for two people to bow to one another. The depth of the bow, however, indicates dominance or submission. In a work environment an employee might bow halfway for an immediate supervisor or manager, but bow all the way toward the floor for the CEO or company president. The bow was used as a signal between samurai rivals in ancient Japan, with many a conflict erupting due to the perceived insult of a bow that was not low enough or respectful enough.

In the Western world, body lowering appears in the form of kneeling down, performing a curtsy, bowing the head, or sitting down. Remember how it used to be considered polite for a man to tip his hat to a woman or to a person of higher status? This was a form of body lowering, making the person appear to lower himself by removing his hat and reducing his height. The military salute is rooted in the tipping of hats, where the hand movement to the forehead symbolizes removing a hat before a higher ranking person.

You will often see children using body lowering behavior when being disciplined or lectured by an adult. The child will sink down into a chair or maybe even sit on the floor as a signal of submission to the adult. Most adults even do this from time to time as well, whether in the workplace, during a group activity, or when faced with their own parents.

Averting eyes. Direct eye contact is a sign of confidence, but too much direct eye contact is perceived as a challenge or as aggression. Going back to the animal world for a moment, when two rival bobcats confront each other their eyes lock together and neither one wants to look away because looking away is a submissive signal.

In humans, averting the eyes often shows up during courtship behavior. A woman will make brief eye contact with a man and then avert her eyes and look away, sending the signal that she is open to him initiating contact with her. Or, if you are sitting in a meeting and the boss begins to criticize or chastise someone, that person might avert his or her eyes in submission to what the boss is saying. Most of the other people in the room will probably avert their eyes as well, showing their submission and desire not to become an object of criticism.

Children who have a staring contest are effectively challenging each other for dominance and submission. The one who looks away first is dubbed the loser, with the winner taking on more control and dominance. This is especially common between siblings, where the older child wants to maintain dominance and the younger child wants to gain some dominance. The two of them will have a staring contest to see who will end up in the submissive position.

Moving away. You've probably had someone, maybe a teacher or a parent, at some point in your life tell you to just walk away when someone tried to start an argument or pick a fight with you. Why?

Because moving away is a signal of submission, clearly communicating you are not willing to engage in conflict.

When you move away from another person, either backing away or stepping aside to let someone pass, you're essentially giving up your space or position and allowing the other person to claim that space or position. Even if it's only for a moment, the movement to create more distance is a sign of submission.

Once again, children provide an excellent real-world example of this. When two children are arguing, wrestling, or otherwise challenging each other, eventually one of them will try to get away from the other one. The child may run across the playground, go into the bedroom and close the door, or just slowly back away.

Adults do this same thing when driving a car. What happens when you are driving along and another person tries to merge into your lane? If that person appears to be evaluating your speed and slowing enough to merge in behind you, there's generally not a problem. However, if that person appears to be trying to match or exceed your speed to cut in front of you, that creates a choice for you. Do you speed up even more to keep the other car from beating you and getting in front? Or do you consciously slow down and create more space in front of you, letting the other person have their little victory because it's not worth a larger confrontation?

Uncertainty

The body language of uncertainty is generally pretty obvious. There is a tentativeness and a hesitancy that emanate from someone who is uncertain about something. The classic nonverbal signals of uncertainty are darting eyes and hesitant movements.

Darting eyes. You've probably done this hundreds if not thousands of times in your life. You're not sure which road to follow, so your eyes dart back and forth looking for a street sign or some indication of the correct place to turn. Or, you and a friend are meeting for coffee and you find yourself at the coffee shop but your friend isn't there. Are you at the wrong place? You begin looking around, checking faces and watching the door, hoping your friend will appear and relieve your uncertainty.

This nonverbal behavior is easy to see in nearly any airport you might visit. As passengers disembark from a plane, the ones who are not familiar with the airport start moving their eyes around, searching for something to guide them in the right direction. It might be a sign pointing toward the baggage claim or a display screen showing the gate number for their connecting flight. You'll know right away when they find something to reassure them and point them in the right direction, because their eyes will stop moving around and they'll focus in a particular direction.

Hesitant movements. This is sort of a catch-all term to describe movements that are not smooth or steady. When you feel uncertainty, chances are you will not just charge forward and take action. Instead, you proceed cautiously and carefully, trying to figure things out along the way. This may show up as small, irregular steps in one or more directions; fidgeting in your seat or chair; a shaky tone of voice; or even shaking or sweating hands.

Let's go back to the airport example for a moment. You've already seen people darting their eyes around looking for information, but they're probably showing hesitant movements as well. They take a step or two in one direction, stop, then a step or two another direction, with these careful steps slowly evolving into a steady stride as certainty grows.

Here's another example. Have you ever watched someone jump off the high dive at a swimming pool for the first time? There are usually lots of hesitant movements to see in that situation, perhaps starting with several starts and stops on the way over to the ladder. Climbing the ladder might occur slowly, and once up on top, the person will probably grasp the hand rail and carefully inch his way out to the edge. If the person is especially uncertain about making the jump, he might go back and forth a few times, mentally working up the certainty and confidence to jump in.

Confidence

Confident body language is also relatively easy to observe; it is also one of the easiest nonverbal behaviors to fake when you really don't feel very confident at all. A confident person generally walks with a smooth, steady stride, not hesitating or pausing along the way. The body posture is upright, with shoulders back, head up, and eyes focused ahead. The hands are steady and the tone of voice is steady as well.

Think about the last time you felt especially confident about something, perhaps your work performance or your knowledge going into a classroom quiz. What kind of body language did you show? If you're not sure, ask someone who observed you in that situation to describe the way you looked and acted. In some cases, the other person might describe you as appearing not at all confident, in which case you need to do a bit more thinking about the mismatch between your inner thoughts and your external nonverbal cues.

I said earlier that confidence can be faked, which you have probably done at some point in your life as well. For instance, think about the first day on a new job. You were scared, excited, nervous, and anxious all at the same time, but since you wanted to make a really great first impression you consciously assumed an upright posture, kept your head up, and did your best to walk smoothly down the hallway.

Have you ever heard the phrase "Fake it until you make it"? It means you should deliberately choose the necessary behaviors to show confidence in yourself, and if you do that often enough and long enough that confidence will eventually develop for real. Sales training programs often use a variation of this, teaching salespeople to approach every client interaction as if their product or service is the best possible solution for the client. Whether that confidence is warranted or not, just using those confident behaviors will help convince the client you're right and help move the client along toward making a purchase.

Personal Identity

This last category, personal identity, brings together elements from several categories to create an overall impression. Your internal definition of your personal identity comes through in your body language, either consciously or unconsciously. It becomes your signature of sorts, kind of like a self-fulfilling prophecy.

For instance, let's say your personal identity is all about being an athlete. You see yourself as an athlete and you enjoy athletic activities, so those elements start appearing in your body language. You might stretch and flex your muscles every so often, or turn toward the sound of a sporting event on TV. Perhaps you walk with confidence or sometimes jog slightly on the way out to your car in the parking lot. When you are around other athletic people you probably start to match their nonverbal behaviors, too, so that all of you are sending body language messages about your personal identities as athletes.

Another case of personal identity affecting body language is the example of the schoolyard bully. Deep inside, he lacks confidence in some way, so to avoid letting that show he chooses an aggressive, bullying personal identity. You'll see dominant behavior and attempts to increase status, as well as all of the nonverbal cues that go along with them. The bully creates this identity of a tough person and communicates it through body language rather than run the risk of letting others see inside his deeper fears.

Remember, your body language is constantly communicating information about you—attitudes, feeling, thoughts, emotions, and so forth. At various times of the day you may cycle through all of the categories I've covered in this chapter, depending on situations and circumstances you encounter. When you are aware of what your body language says about you, it's much easier to make conscious choices about keeping, altering, or abandoning nonverbal behaviors to help you achieve whatever it is you want to achieve.

Chapter 6 TAKEAWAYS

1. Your body language is constantly communicating information about you such as thoughts, feelings, emotions, attitude, self-confidence, and so on.

2. The nonverbal messages you send generally fall into one or more of six main categories:

    Status

    Dominance

    Submission

    Uncertainty

    Confidence

    Personal identity

3. Status is characterized by messages related to height. This shows up in nonverbal cues such as posture, touch, and location.

4. Dominance is similar to status but relates more to power and control within individual interactions and relationships. It shows up in nonverbal cues such as elevation, hand position, and body movement.

5. Submission is on the opposite end of the spectrum from dominance, relating to allowing someone else to assume the dominant role. It shows up in nonverbal cues such as body lowering, averting the eyes, and moving away.

6. Uncertainty is generally fairly easy to see in terms of body language; it is a message of being hesitant, tentative, or

unsettled about something. It shows up in nonverbal cues such as darting eyes and hesitant movements.

7. Body language demonstrating confidence is also generally easy to observe; it is also the kind of body language that can be faked when necessary. It shows up in nonverbal cues such as steady walking strides, upright posture, head up, and eyes focused ahead.

8. Personal identity brings together several elements from other categories to create an overall impression. You have an internal definition of your personal identity that affects your body language. Your body language becomes much like a signature of your personal identity and/or a self-fulfilling prophecy of sorts.

Chapter 6 WORKSHEET

1. Review the Chapter 6 Takeaways and answer the following:
   - Which key point(s) did you find most interesting? Why?
   - Which key point(s) did you find most surprising? Why?

2. Think about situations where you have exhibited body language and nonverbal cues for each of the six main categories. Describe your actions and the effect of those actions on the perceptions others have of you.

   Status

   Dominance

   Submission

   Uncertainty

   Confidence

   Personal identity

7

Personal Interactions

A t this point in the book you have been exposed to a broad foundation of information about body language, and now it's time to put that information to work. It's time to focus on even more practical applications for the types of interactions you encounter every day. You'll still pick up some academic pieces of information, of course, but my intent is to take you through the most common applications of body language and nonverbal behavior study in real life.

Appearance

There is no overestimating the power of appearance.

Women who are more attractive are perceived by both men and women to be more intelligent, caring, and better at parenting.

Men who are tall possess a big advantage in many ways over men who are not when it comes to competing for the attention of women.

Women are strongly drawn to attractive men, but outside of a one-night stand or short-term sexual relationship, men who are attractive and possess other characteristics of status or dominance are met with unconscious resistance.

A man can be too perfect.

The reason should be obvious.

If the man scores a 10 in too many categories he will have the attention of all the women who are out there looking for the short-term sexual affair but perhaps not the long-term relationship.

First Impressions

Every time you meet someone for the first time your body language communicates volumes about you and provides the other person with the raw materials needed to form an immediate judgment about you. It may not be politically correct and few, if any, people will admit to it in polite society, but the fact remains: Body language speaks louder than words.

In just a few seconds and often before you've spoken a full sentence, others decide if you are friendly, if you are courteous, if you are submissive, and what status should be accorded you, among other things. Let's take a look, then, at what you can do to maximize the positives of the first impressions you make.

If possible, double-check your clothing and general neatness before meeting the other person. You want to appear clean and neat, not sloppy and unkempt. Make firm eye contact and walk up to the other person with confidence.

Smile, say hello, and reach out to shake hands.

Stand about four feet away and turn very slightly sideways (if you face the other person directly that is often interpreted as dominant or competitive). If the two of you choose to sit down, sit up straight (not stiff) and keep an open body posture.

This is, of course, a very general guideline. You can make subtle changes depending on whether you are meeting someone in a business situation, a social situation, or someone of equal status or of some other status. There are literally thousands of variations you might encounter so the most important thing to remember is to be conscious of your body language in first impression situations. Don't operate on autopilot, but instead give some deliberate thought to how you can make the best impression possible in the given situation.

Building Rapport

Building rapport is very much like a dance. You and your partner meet in the middle and then negotiate your way through a variety of steps. At some point you agree on a set of steps and start using them to move smoothly wherever you want to go on the dance floor.

Rapport is critical for so many kinds of personal interactions, whether you're meeting with a client, a friend, a stranger, a relative, or anyone else. Real, honest communication can only begin once you and the other person have agreed upon the steps you're going to use and start using them to interact.

The basic idea behind building rapport is to find common ground and shared ideas because let's face it: You would rather interact with someone very much like yourself. This is a natural human desire and something everyone does to one degree or another, but if you learn the key steps to developing rapport you can apply them in nearly any situation.

So what are these key steps? They include the following:

- **Mirroring**—your body language, your movements, your posture, your tone of voice, your style of dress.

- **Listening**—ask open-ended questions and listen for key wants and needs, check for understanding.

- **Reciprocating**—similar pressure when shaking hands, taking turns opening doors, offering actions or items of similar value.

The specific actions you take will vary depending on the situation, but if you stay within these three main categories you'll do well.

Establishing Trust

Establishing trust expands upon rapport and transforms an interaction to an even higher level of communication. Trust is an integral part of all relationships, and while rapport can be developed in a relatively short time, trust must be developed over a longer length of time.

Trust emerges over time as you clearly demonstrate to each other genuine concern for the other's well-being and the fulfillment of promises and agreements. The components of establishing trust are the same as establishing rapport, but with slightly different nuances and degrees of honesty.

- **Mirroring**—your tone of voice, the way you greet each other, your degree of leaning toward each other, eye contact, head nodding.

- **Listening**—keep information exchanges confidential, honor differences, check for understanding, find areas of common ground, hear what is really being said.

- **Reciprocating**—sharing similar levels of information, responding to a gesture of trust with another gesture of trust, anticipating needs and offering support.

Trust takes longer to establish than rapport, but it can be destroyed much more rapidly. In a romantic relationship, for example, flirting with another person or attempting too much physical contact can damage trust almost immediately. In a business relationship, to give an additional example, you can quickly lose the trust of a client if you don't fulfill a commitment. Friendships are another area where trust is so important, especially among women who tend to share deeper emotions and feelings with each other.

Reading Messages

Body language tells you a great deal about the messages another person is sending. Their nonverbal behaviors allow you to compare their words to their body language to help determine truth, honesty, deception, sincerity, enthusiasm, and so on. When you successfully read their body language you can much more accurately evaluate their overall message.

Two nonverbal behaviors are particularly important when reading messages:

- **Eye contact.** This is a big part of reading another person because it is the thing that we tend to notice most easily and most immediately. When the other person makes appropriate eye contact you find him more trustworthy; while shifting eyes, looking down or away, or avoiding eye contact altogether creates the opposite effect in your interpretation.

- **Body movement.** A person who is nervously bouncing a leg, leaning or turning away from you, or moving in too close to you takes away from his words and puts the focus on his body language. You may doubt the information, question his honesty, or find him too pushy or aggressive.

Think about this the next time you interact with another person. Pay attention to how body language affects your interpretation of the message. You just might be surprised at how much influence it really has on you.

Sending Messages

Just as body language is integral to reading messages from other people, it is also critical to the effectiveness of the messages you send to others. Sometimes your nonverbal behaviors are unconscious, while other times you deliberately choose them in order to influence the sending of a message.

A job interview is a great example of a time when you are acutely aware of your body language and the messages it sends. You walk in the room confidently and reach out to shake hands, you sit up straight at the table, and of course you make good eye contact as you answer questions. However, your inadvertent body language can also show up during a job interview. Your hands might sweat or shake, your voice might quiver, or you may struggle to make good eye contact but instead look down or look away.

Mediators and dispute resolution experts are extremely conscious of their body language when working with other parties. They will make a point of using equal eye contact with each side, showing open body language to both sides, and avoid nodding or head shaking when others are talking. Their body language also sends important messages when a conflict gets heated or intense. A calm voice, relaxed body position, and downward hand gestures can help to diffuse a tense situation.

A great way to spot your own nonverbal behaviors and how they affect your messages is to videotape yourself during an interaction. You should, of course, ask the other person's permission before recording, but most people are happy to agree when you let them know you are working on improving your communication skills. When the interaction is finished, go back and look at the tape, taking notes on your observations. Even better, put the tape away for a few days and then look at it again. You'll probably notice even more the second time around.

Sending Strong Messages that Will Last

This is one of the most important intentional uses of body language and nonverbal communication you will use.

Eventually you'll do it with no awareness.

You're at work (for the purpose of getting stuff done or you'd be at home with people you prefer to be with).

You don't want to be bothered.

Especially by the people who take two hours to say something that takes two minutes.

You can't always say, "Get out of here, can't you see I'm working?"

What to do?

Continue working on your project.

Look at your computer screen.

Don't lift your eyes away from the screen except to compare notes with documents on your desk.

Look angry.

Look intense.

Make all of your movements sharp (as opposed to easy, calm, and relaxed).

Look like you could kill the idiot who caused *this*.

(Continue working.)

No one will come near you.

And that's what you want and need.

Privacy and the ability to think while you work without distraction.

Your question: "What if they don't get it and come in anyway?"

Good question.

As they walk in the door, continue to scroll down on the screen on your computer.

Look at a document down and to the right.

Continue to look intense and angry.

Raise the tensed index finger of your left hand slowly up and away from your body toward the person entering your office.

Look back to the computer screen.

Hold your finger in suspended animation.

Shake your head.

Say, "idiots."

Slowly lower your index finger and as you do, slowly move your gaze to the person, not changing the expression on your face.

"Idiots. Hi John, what can I do for you?"

Keep the angry and intense look on your face.

Glare right into John's eyes.

Say nothing else.

Hold this position.

John will say one to three sentences if not, "I'll come back later."

Your time at work is something you probably don't cherish.

You probably would rather be with your spouse or children or at the club.

Always be kind to your coworkers, but feel free to be angry toward that computer screen.

For Your Sanity

The most effective "Do Not Disturb" sign is to have your eyes closed, breath coming slowly and deeply and your arms crossed over your chest.

They will leave you alone.

Deception

The role of body language in deception is the subject of a great deal of research and investigation. It is not only valuable in terms of interpersonal relationships but also has very practical applications in society, too. Lie detectors are a good example of how body language can be measured to help indicate degrees of deception.

Some nonverbal behaviors are obvious and common indicators of deception such as darting eyes, exaggerated facial expressions, or shifting weight back and forth. Others are not so obvious and require close attention to spot. If you've ever played poker you probably know what I mean by this. Poker is at its heart a game of deception and most players have nonverbal cues that reveal when they are bluffing. Professionals call these cues "tells" and go to great lengths to read those of others while hiding their own.

Children have an especially hard time keeping their body language under control when attempting to deceive someone because they have not had enough life experience to develop that control. Most parents can tell immediately when a child is attempting deception by a combination of their words and their body language. They tend to look down and avoid eye contact or sometimes make excessive eye contact and try very hard to convince you of their earnestness. A child might have trouble sitting or standing still during deception, and those with really tender hearts may break down sobbing right in the middle and admit what they were really trying to do.

The Lie

Detecting deception is no easy task.

There are different kinds of deception and there are different degrees of deception.

Some kinds of deception like omission occur when someone doesn't tell you something that is important. They leave it out.

"I was at the bar last night, honey."

vs.

"I was at the bar last night honey, and then I met this woman who . . ."

There are also errors of commission.

"This car has never been in a car accident."

(It actually has—twice.)

The first key point you need to understand is that not all lies are evident in nonverbal behavior. There are zero clues or cues for many lies.

Some people are good liars. Some people are pathological liars. Some people rehearse what their story will be over and over so it comes naturally.

Other times when people lie there *are* cues and clues.

There are a number of things I look for when I think someone might be deceiving me.

The most important cue is usually expressed by their feet.

People generally have no trouble controlling their torso, even their hand gestures and sometimes facial changes. But one thing that is hard for the liar to pay attention to is feet!

When communicating with someone, I gain a sense for how his feet normally move in conversation. When someone attempts to deceive, his feet behave differently. That's my best and probably most reliable cue.

Next up, I watch pupil changes. Some people's pupils get bigger; some people's get smaller. I'm not so concerned about the direction of the size change (bigger vs. smaller). I'm interested that there is or is not a change.

The third thing I look for are expressions of boredom, indifference, and unconcern. These are tough states to fake for most people because they are typically unaware of their behavior. In young people, this collection of vocal and nonverbal cues is even more obvious to the receiver.

The liar will try to look indifferent but because he isn't used to behaving indifferently he is trying to guess what he should be acting like. Unfortunately for him, it's usually a dead giveaway.

If people stumble over their words, repeat phrases or words, especially when this is not their normal behavior, this is a fairly useful tell as well.

On the other hand, if someone is on trial in the Kevin Hogan Mind Court, there are some things that I look for to establish "innocence."

First, can or does the person give a genuine smile. It is hard to give a real smile when you are lying to someone. Obviously, the pathological liar can, but absent a pathological liar, it takes a genuine actor to smile convincingly and lie at the same time.

Next, I'm looking for "verbal immediacy." Does the person answer me quickly and normally? It's tough to lie and communicate quickly. The faster you talk the less time there is to process information. When you're lying it takes time to process information to make sure the story comes out right. This doesn't mean that people who respond slowly are lying. It means that coupled with other innocence cues, I become more convinced whether someone is telling the truth or lying to me.

Most people can't determine whether someone is lying or not with any degree of accuracy. When crossing cultural lines it's even more difficult to accurately assess whether someone is being truthful or not.

Sometimes experienced police officers show better than chance accuracy in detecting deception but typically most people can't figure out truth vs. lie more than 55 percent of the time.

The reason is that people are looking at the wrong things.

They look at eye contact.

Fact is that eye contact isn't all that relevant in determining whether most people are lying or telling the truth.

Another cue people look for is nervousness, and yes, nervousness is slightly correlated to lying, but it's also correlated to being scared and afraid of being accused of lying!

Want to have a good guess as to whether someone is telling the truth of lying to you?

Record the conversation and then listen to it when you aren't in the presence of the person. People who can't see the person who is talking usually are better at detecting truth vs. lie. Why? The vocal cues are some of the strongest to pick up on.

Because it is such a well-kept secret in the nonverbal community, there is one powerful strategy you can use to improve your odds of detecting deception.

Liars must construct their stories in chronological order. People who tell the truth will be all over the map.

The liar has to create a story, remember it in order, and tell it chronologically. Because there is no actual memory to recall, the liar has developed a false memory.

The truth teller might often sound like a liar because he is all over the map, but the fact is that is more likely to be a sign of truth than fiction.

Ask the person what happened in reverse chronological order. The liar won't be able to do it most of the time.

Affection

This is a part of body language that you know and use automatically and without thinking, in most cases. It is preprogrammed into human beings as a way to promote bonding and family groups. In the modern world, our nonverbal behaviors to show affection are just as important and just as critical to our lives.

Affectionate body language includes touching, leaning in, making body contact with a shoulder or arm, tilting the head down and looking upwards, facial expressions, and drawing the object of affection in closer. This is just a short list; there are many other nonverbal signs of affection both deliberate and spontaneous.

I don't have a foot fetish (one of those things I never understood) but people who pay attention to other people's feet have a clue about what's going on in their heads.

When people's feet are pointed toward or near someone, they probably have positive feelings for them. When people's feet are pointed away from someone they unconsciously tell us they want to leave.

Pay attention to people who have their feet on the way out the door but the body still directed at the person they're trying to get away from.

The other interesting thing to watch for in feet is when a person is seated, and they are faced with a potentially anxiety-provoking conversation. If people keep their feet apart they probably are okay with the situation. If they cross their ankles and/or seem to apply pressure or tension from one ankle to the other, you can bet they are not comfortable.

Let's look at just one of these in more detail—touching. Now, you probably touch other people several times a day but many of those contacts are not designed to convey affection. Perhaps you tap someone on the shoulder to get their attention or bump into someone when sitting down on the bus or train. What is it, then, that makes touch change from neutral to affectionate?

Intent. Your intent when touching is an underlying factor in showing affection. If you want to show affection then you will look for ways to touch another person in gentle ways, in friendly ways, and often in ways that linger just a moment or two longer than is necessary. Playfulness is also a sign of affectionate intent, such as when a woman gently elbows a man with whom she is flirting or a man finds an excuse to put his arm around a woman.

Firmness. A firm touch conveys a completely different message than a soft, gentle touch. Placing a hand on a shoulder and resting it lightly can be a sign of affection as can gently touching or holding another person's hand. In general, the lighter and smoother a touch is, the more likely it is to be intended and interpreted as affection.

Duration. The duration of touch is a powerful indicator of affection. If a touch lasts longer than normal for a particular circumstance or situation, affection is a likely interpretation. You might shake hands and let the clasp continue for a few seconds longer than normal, or you might rest your hand on the other person's arm as you lean in to look at something they want to show you.

Anger

Body language is a powerful part of expressing anger. You might look at another person with daggers in your eyes, scowl darkly, move closer with your body, stand up straighter and taller with your chest out, or shake your fist vigorously. All of these are nonverbal behaviors that clearly communicate to another person that you are angry.

When you are angry at another person your body language is generally directed at that person. You turn to look at them, you walk toward them, you point at them, and so forth. But what about when you are angry with yourself, a situation, an occurrence, or something other than another person? In these situations your body language probably changes a bit, both consciously and subconsciously. You may grind your teeth together, clench and unclench your fists, purse your lips, bounce your foot, breathe loudly or more frequently, or change your facial expression.

Let's again look at just one of these in more detail—facial expression. Your face is truly a window into your emotions and your messages, sometimes deliberately and sometimes spontaneously. You might scowl in mock anger to make a point, or clench your teeth and smile at the same time to express anger in a more humorous way. The parts of your face work together and interact with each other to communicate anger to others.

Mouth. Your mouth shows anger by tensing up. Your lips may press firmly together, for instance, or you might curl up one side of your mouth in a sneer. Another common mouth behavior is to push your chin forward and purse your lips together and slightly outward.

Eyes/Eyebrows. Eyes express anger spontaneously by contracting the pupils. You may also squint slightly to make your eyes appear smaller and more menacing. Eyebrows that are furrowed, drawn together, or creating vertical lines in the forehead also express anger.

Facial Muscles. Your face has 22 muscles on each side, all of which interact to express different information about your mood and your emotions. In general, your facial muscles will become tense and hard when you are angry as opposed to relaxed and soft when you are happy.

Intimacy

Body language and nonverbal behaviors communicate intimacy as well as foster intimacy. A woman who brushes her hand against another communicates a feeling of intimacy, while a leader who sets up chairs in a circle rather than around a table fosters intimacy within a group of people.

Power Reading Point

When you know that two people are in a relationship with each other:

If the man touches the women more, the relationship is not likely to be a committed one.

If the woman touches the man more often, the relationship is likely to be more committed.

Tidbit: Men tend to touch women with their hands, whereas women tend to touch others with other parts of their bodies.

People often associate intimacy with sexuality, probably because the word "intimate" is frequently used as a polite euphemism for sex. True intimacy, however, does not have to be sexual and, in fact, is more often not sexual at all. The Encarta dictionary lists several other meanings for intimacy, including:

- A close personal relationship.

- A quiet and private atmosphere.

- Detailed knowledge due to close or long association or study.

- A private or personal action or statement.

It's worth noting that these four meanings are listed ahead of sex, offering a powerful insight into the broad scope and nature of intimacy. Let's look at how body language can communicate each of these types of intimacy.

A close personal relationship: sitting close together, leaning in toward each other, friendly and relaxed facial expressions and gestures.

A quiet and private atmosphere: open body posture, relaxed body position, slow and smooth movements, smiling, and quiet tone of voice.

Detailed knowledge due to close or long association or study: confident movements, giving firm direction through pushing or pulling on an arm, sitting close together, listening and nodding.

A private or personal action or statement: listening and nodding, leaning in close to speak, focused eye contact, gentle touch on the hand or arm.

Do you see yourself in any of these descriptions? How do you use body language and nonverbal behaviors in each of these situations? If you're not sure, pay attention to yourself the next time you have an interaction such as these and notice how your body language communicates and contributes to a sense of intimacy.

Touching Others

Men are much less likely to touch others than women; and women touch other women more than they do men.

The Complex Formula for Succeeding in Getting Attention from the Opposite Sex

Research in the real world combined with the solid data available online will give you a clear picture of what women want—and it's almost all nonverbal.

Most of the data in this section of the book is derived from the MIT Sloan School of Management.

The impact of attractiveness is powerful.

Research of online dating web sites uncovers some sobering realities:

Attractiveness

Men in the top 5 percent of attractiveness receive twice as many first contacts as the next 5 percent of attractiveness. Some women may truly believe looks don't matter to them . . . but they do.

Men in the fourth decile get twice as many first contacts as those in the lowest decile.

The same is true for women.

Height

Men in the 6'3"–6'4" category receive two-thirds more first contact e-mail than men in the 5'7"–5'9" category.

Women in the 5'3"–5'8" range receive the most first contact e-mail, and it goes down sharply as the woman gets taller.

Weight

When it comes to how much body weight is on that frame (how thin or obese someone is), we find some surprises and some expectations met.

Men whose body mass index (BMI) is 27 (slightly overweight but not by much, get the most first contact e-mail. Women whose BMI is 17 get the most first contact e-mail. Supermodels have BMIs of 17.

The woman with a BMI of 25 gets half the first contact e-mail of one whose BMI is 17.

Hair

As far as hair color, blondes do receive a bit more first contact e-mail then do brown-haired women. Women with gray and salt-and-pepper hair receive much less first contact e-mail.

Men with long curly hair get significantly less first contact e-mail than those with straight, medium-length hair.

For women?

Long, straight hair gets more first contact e-mail than does short hair.

Ethnicity

Thirty-eight percent of women prefer to meet someone in their own ethnic background. Only 18 percent of men express such a preference.

African-American and Hispanic men get only half as many first-contact e-mails from Caucasian women as do Caucasian men; Asian men get only about one-quarter as many.

An African-American man in the United States must earn $154,000 more than a Caucasian man to receive the same number of contacts as a Caucasian man. Hispanic men are required to earn $77,000 more than Caucasian men for the same number of first contacts and Asian-American men must earn $247,000 more than Caucasian men to get the same amount of first contact e-mail.

The income compensation experiment didn't work for women, because men aren't as interested in that variable in mate seeking. An African-American woman would need to be an 8 out of 10 in attractiveness to be as successful with Caucasian men as a 5 out of 10 Caucasian woman.

Trading Height for Money

Using a 5′11″ man with a $62,500 income and in the 40 to 50 percent decile of attractiveness as a baseline, here are the adjustments in annual income and height that are required by women in the top half of attractiveness.

$$5'0'' = \$317,000$$
$$5'2'' = \$269,000$$
$$5'4'' = \$221,000$$
$$5'6'' = \$175,000$$
$$5'8'' = \$138,000$$
$$5'10'' = \$24,000$$
$$6'0'' = -\$28,000$$
$$6'2'' = -\$30,000$$
$$6'4'' = -\$51,000$$
$$6'6'' = -\$63,000$$
$$6'10'' = -\$63,000$$

We now know that there is indeed a looks/income trade-off as well that women consider.

If an average-looking man wants to have a woman in the top 10 percent of attractiveness, he will need to earn $186,000 more per year than his friend who ranks 9.5 (out of 10) in attractiveness and earns $62,500.

The amount of money a woman makes is not important to a man when looking for a mate.

Does Anything Else Matter?

Yes.

Women who walk with those swaying Marilyn Monroe hips increase their perceived physical attractiveness by about 50 percent.

Men who walk with a swagger in their step can double (yes double) their attractiveness to women.

A little movement can go a long way!

Problem: When you're seated . . .

Separation

You can use body language as an extremely powerful and visible sign of separation from someone or something else. It is a clear way to distance yourself from something that's uncomfortable for you, meets with your disapproval, or violates your personal code of conduct.

For instance, if you are in a group of people and one member of the group speaks too loudly, says something insulting, or otherwise creates a scene, your body language might include looking away, a frowning facial expression, leaning back away from the person, taking a step or two away, or even turning your back to that person.

Couples use body language to show they are linked to each other, and they also use body language to show when that link has been dissolved. They may turn away from each other when in a group of people or make a point of walking on opposite sides of the hallway from each other. Eye contact may be brief or avoided entirely. All of these nonverbal cues communicate to each other and to the rest of the world that they are no longer a couple and do not wish to be perceived as linked together.

Teenagers are experts at using body language to show separation from their parents. They roll their eyes, they turn their backs, and they walk several feet away from their parents in the mall or on the street. When a parent says something, teens may shrug to show disinterest or disagreement as a way to demonstrate they are separate from their parent.

Chapter 7 **TAKEAWAYS**

1. Body language is an integral part of personal interactions. It can be used deliberately to influence an interaction or can appear spontaneously. Either way, studying body language and nonverbal behaviors has many practical applications for real life.

2. First impressions are influenced by body language through your posture, your facial expressions, your distance from another person, your clothing, and your eye contact.

3. Building rapport is influenced by mirroring, listening, and reciprocating. It can be developed within a relatively short amount of time.

4. Establishing trust expands upon rapport to create higher levels of communication. It is also influenced by mirroring, listening, and reciprocating, but with slightly different nuances.

5. Reading messages is influenced by how you perceive and interpret the body language and nonverbal cues of the person sending the message. Two key aspects are eye contact and body movement.

6. Sending messages of your own requires attention to your own body language. You may deliberately choose your body language such as during a job interview, but you will likely

still have spontaneous body language that you can see when you videotape yourself.

7. Deception and body language are extremely interconnected. Detecting deception by observing nonverbal behaviors is a focus of scientific research, but is also a skill used when playing games, parenting, and so on.

8. Affection is expressed through body language both deliberate and spontaneous. For example, touching is perceived as affectionate based on your intent, its firmness, and its duration.

9. Anger is commonly expressed through body language, whether that anger is directed at someone else, at yourself, at a situation, or the like. For example, your facial expressions are a combination of your mouth, your eyes, eyebrows, and your facial muscles.

10. Intimacy is expressed through a variety of body language, most often in ways that are not sexual. Your nonverbal behaviors may communicate intimacy as well as create intimacy, depending on the situation and how you apply them.

11. Separation is expressed through body language by turning away, moving away, or otherwise avoiding the perception of linkage with something else. You may express separation due to discomfort, disapproval, violation of personal values, and so on.

Chapter 7 WORKSHEET

1. Review the Chapter 7 Takeaways and answer the following:
   - Which key point(s) did you find most interesting? Why?
   - Which key point(s) did you find most surprising? Why?

2. Think about your own body language in personal interactions. Write down an example of how you have used or perceived body language in each of these real-life situations:

Building rapport

Establishing trust

Reading messages

Sending messages

Deception

Affection

Anger

Intimacy

Separation

8

The Secret Language of Influence in Business

M ost of my speaking events in 2007 were to teach employees, salespeople and upper management of large companies how to use body language to be more influential.

If no one has shown your people how to effectively influence others with a primary focus on the context, environment and non-verbal communication, this is the biggest untapped resource in your company.

I used to tell people how much money companies make after implementing changes, but the numbers are so ridiculously out of line with standard training or speakers, I literally quit doing it.

The Secret Language of Business is nowhere more important or profitable than at the office and in the field.

Let your salespeople learn how to understand nonverbal cues and they become confident. Let them learn how to send "buying messages," and they increase sales . . . a lot.

A great deal of research and study is focused on the effects and practical applications of body language and nonverbal behaviors in the world of business. Everything from the way you dress to the way you walk to the way you talk have influence on your business interactions, often in ways that might surprise or even horrify you. In this chapter I'll take you through the basics of body language in the general business environment and then go into more detail about specific business situations—meetings, selling, hiring, peer-to-peer interactions, and manager-to-subordinate interactions.

The Business Environment

The business environment is a world all its own, filled with norms, nuance, contradiction, and competition. Negotiating your way through this complex maze can be a difficult and frustrating process of learning. Most of that learning comes in the form of on-the-job training where you dive right in and learn valuable lessons by observing others and making your own mistakes along the way.

The body language typically found in the business environment varies depending on the nature of that environment. Four common environments are:

1. Conservative

2. Casual

3. Industrial

4. Academic

In each of these, you will find many different expectations and norms as well as some interesting contradictions. A particular nonverbal behavior in a conservative environment might be accepted and even expected, but in an industrial environment it might be sorely out of place and rejected. Let's look at each of these examples in a bit more detail.

Conservative. This business environment is very traditional, very structured, and very regimented. It is an environment found in a bank, a legal office, or corporate headquarters, just to name a few. The dress is formal, the interactions are controlled and business oriented, and the overall focus is on business rather than people. These are generalities, of course, but tend to be true to one degree or another in a conservative business environment.

If you are in a conservative business environment your body language should be controlled and formal. There should be no loud laughter in the hallways, no walking around whistling and humming a tune, and certainly no spontaneous outbursts of emotion or feelings. Structured and disciplined are probably the best words to describe the expected nonverbal behaviors in this context.

A conservative business environment is really quite superficial in many ways. Everyone practices controlled, deliberate activity, and most pay a great deal of attention to what others think of them and their abilities. You will rarely, if ever, detect emotions or feelings during most interactions, and close, personal friendships are not at all common. Competition is usually an underlying theme in this environment, and it can be brutal at times.

Casual. This business environment is very modern and increasingly common. It is an environment often found in a small or medium-size business, an insurance office, or a consulting firm, just to name a few. The dress is business casual at the most, interactions are more open and genuine, and overall focus is an even split between business and people. Friendships are more common and tend to be more genuine.

If you are in a casual business environment your body language should be less controlled and more informal. It's okay to laugh a bit and socialize a bit to build rapport. There is an understanding, either stated or implied, that a healthy balance between work and home life is encouraged. This is not an excuse to slack or behave in a silly or immature manner, but rather a general feeling of allowing more personal expression as part of fulfilling business expectations.

A casual business environment is much more genuine in most ways. Interactions are less controlled and more authentic, and people feel much more comfortable expressing themselves with enthusiasm and energy. There is often still a sense of competition in a casual business environment, but instead of being an "I win, you lose" approach it is more often an "I'll help you win, you help me win" approach.

Industrial. This business environment is an interesting mix of characteristics. It is usually found in manufacturing companies, repair shops, and construction firms, just to name a few. The dress is usually casual for the administrative and management staff but durable and work related for the rest of the company. Employees in this type of environment usually work in ways that are physically demanding and require specific attention to safety and training.

If you are in an industrial business environment, your body language should be willing, active, and unafraid. It's okay to joke and laugh as long as you are working hard and carrying your fair share of the workload. The workday may be structured around a time clock, or it may be structured around completion of specific tasks or milestones. There is usually a firm dividing line between regular time and overtime, except for management and supervisory personnel.

An industrial business environment is often perceived as a somewhat categorized structure—administration and management in one category and frontline workers in another category. There may be an us vs. them attitude to some extent, but there is often a real sense of comraderie and togetherness, especially among frontline workers. There is often a strong set of norms and expectations for independence as well as mutual support.

Academic. This business environment is another interesting mix of characteristics. It is found at colleges, universities, and think tank organizations, just to name a few. The dress is generally business casual for everyday activities, with some disciplines accepting even very eccentric kinds of clothing. More formal dress is expected for more structured activities, especially for administrators and other members of the leadership group. Employees in this type of work environment may fall into different categories depending on whether they have earned tenure.

If you are in an academic environment, your body language should be fairly open yet thoughtful. Diversity is usually a hallmark of the academic world, in terms of thought, opinion, and background. An exception to this would be seen in a think tank environment that is dedicated to a particular point of view or perspective rather than knowledge and study in general. The workday can vary greatly, and there is usually a great deal of emphasis on study, research, publishing, or the general advancement of knowledge. Interactions may be philosophical and passionate or technical and scientific, depending on the specific discipline or area of focus.

An academic environment is often perceived as liberal, free thinking, independent, or a combination of these and other descriptions. The term "academic freedom" is a real-world issue in this environment, and at the same time there may be pressure to perform in terms of research and publishing.

> **Please Note:** In the more detailed sections that follow I will focus on a typical business environment that is somewhere along the spectrum from conservative to casual.

Meetings

The body language you use in meetings can have a very real impact on the conduct and outcome of those meetings. If you appear fearful or uncertain, the results will likely be vastly different than if you appear confident and informed. When you are conscious of your body language and nonverbal behaviors, you can dramatically influence the meeting process.

Where you sit. Take a seat at the head of the table if you are the leader or in charge of running the meeting, but otherwise select a seat somewhere along the sides. If there is someone in the meeting who you find difficult or with whom you are likely to disagree, try not to take a seat directly across from that person because that sets up a very competitive, confrontational body posture.

How you sit. Sit with an upright posture not with a slouch. Lean slightly forward if you like, but don't lean casually on the table. If you keep your arms on the table, rest them in a slightly open position with fingers together and refrain from playing with your pen, pencil, or paper. If you keep your arms off the table, rest them on the arms of the chair with your elbows pointed slightly outward. Avoid sitting with your elbows close to your body as this makes you appear timid and afraid.

Should you sit? In some circumstances you shouldn't sit for a meeting at all. If the meeting is short and focused on making a decision of some sort, then stand up for the conversation. This puts you in a more powerful position and also encourages participants to focus on the issue and come to a decision in a timely manner.

Fast Fact

Lazy individuals manipulate objects more than others. However, object manipulation is not seen as a sign of laziness but rather a sign of nervousness or simply being fidgety.

The message received is definitely not always what is being sent.

Control your hands. Keep your fingers together when you gesture with your hands, and keep your gestures small in scope and below the level of your chin. This helps others perceive you as sincere and knowledgeable rather than exaggerated and emotional.

Carry as little as possible. Try not to come to meetings with huge stacks of papers, books, calendars, or an obviously thick and overstuffed briefcase. This creates the perception that you are disorganized and/or a worker bee who does the work assigned by others. Instead, come with a pen, a notepad, and perhaps a handout for others attending the meeting. This creates the perception that you are organized and a capable decision maker.

Follow the ground rules. Most meetings have a set of behavioral ground rules, either written or assumed. If you don't know what they are, ask someone ahead of time so you avoid inadvertently violating them. Even if you don't agree with the ground rules, conduct yourself within their boundaries so that others will pay attention and consider your input. If you deliberately violate the ground rules, others will pay far more attention to your behavior than to your input.

Selling

Your ability to send appropriate body language and accurately read the body language of others is a key component of your ability to sell successfully. It doesn't matter what it is you're selling; it could be a product, a service, even an idea or concept. What's critical is that you use body language and nonverbal cues to help the selling process reach a successful outcome.

Establish rapport. This is important when first getting to know a client, but it is also important when working with a client on a continuing basis. Use mirroring body language, listening body language, and reciprocating body language to put the client at ease with you. Keep your tone of voice calm and unhurried, and ask open-ended questions. Unless the client very obviously wants to make a purchase, you may not want to try selling them at all. There will be plenty of time for that later on.

Minimize gestures. Don't wave your arms, point, or use your hands excessively to make gestures unless it is appropriate for illustrating a process or an activity. Keep your gestures mild and nonthreatening so the client does not feel pressured or intimidated.

Choose the appropriate relative position. By this I mean you should consider carefully where you sit or where you stand when working with a client. If you are just getting to know the client, let him sit in the power position with his back to a wall and your back to the door.

If you are negotiating price, don't sit squarely opposite each other in a competitive posture.

Never take a position relative to the other person so that he feels trapped, intimidated, or pressured.

Use your voice as a nonverbal tool. Many people who sell something for a living spend a lot of time talking with clients and potential clients on the phone. In those situations your body language is not visible to the other person so you may be tempted to slouch back, put your feet up, or treat the conversation too casually. Remember that your body language influences your voice and its impact as a nonverbal tool, so use the same behaviors you would in person. Stand up or sit up straight, smile, use a comfortable hand gesture, and so on, because all of these come through quite clearly in your voice.

The Most Important Lesson I Ever Learned in Nonverbal Communication

Learning this has made me hundreds of thousands of dollars.

If your counterpart is right-handed, you will be received better and have a far greater likelihood of making the sale if you are seated off to that person's right.

This extraordinary phenomenon is little known and took me completely by surprise one afternoon when I was teaching high-level executives at the University of St. Thomas in

Minneapolis how to use nonverbal communication to make sales and create more productive work environments.

What happens is that when right-handed people look to the left, they tend to activate more of the right brain in contrast to the left. This means the person will shortly feel anxiety, fear, or nervousness that is not readily explained.

When right-handed people look to the right, they tend to activate more of the left brain. This is predictive of people feeling more at ease, comfortable, and relaxed.

The full explanation of why this occurs is a complex neurological phenomenon and you can read about it at www.kevinhogan.com/theright.htm

For now, simply know that the right brain is home to autobiographical and emotionally charged memories. Most of those memories are very disconcerting and easily activated under stress.

There is also a lengthy discussion of how to communicate to left-handed people to put them at ease in the second half of the article.

The rule I teach people is that "right eyes lining up when you say hello, makes everything all right."

If your right-handed counterpart is ever looking off to his left for an extended period of time you can predict with certainty he will feel very uncomfortable and you will almost certainly lose the sale, respect, or focus of the individual.

Hiring

When you are in the position of hiring, your body language is a powerful part of the process. It doesn't matter if you are the ultimate decision maker or if you are a member of the interview panel, your nonverbal behaviors still have an important influence. They influence the person being interviewed, they affect the quality of the information you uncover during the hiring process, and they create an important first impression for the potential new hire.

Use an open body posture. Your job during the interview process is to uncover the information you need to make a decision about which person to hire, and, in order to do that, you need to use an open body posture to encourage each person to feel as comfortable during the interview as possible. This is not just to be nice; it is a specific method of getting applicants to open up, reveal their true thoughts, and break through the inevitable posturing and superficial behavior that occurs.

Watch for nonverbal cues. Watch the interviewee's nonverbal cues to help you determine when more follow-up questions or greater attention is in order. For instance, if you ask about a previous employer and the interviewee looks away, fidgets, or shows deceptive body language, then you should use follow-up questions rather than simply accepting the first answer.

Watch for too much control. Some people are quite skillful as interviewees, perhaps because they have done a lot of it or because they have received training and coaching. There is nothing wrong with interviewees conducting themselves with polish and professionalism, but when their body language is too controlled and too perfect you might have reason to question them further. Someone who is very controlled at hiding his true position can be a potential problem employee every bit as much as someone who appears deceptive in his answers.

Be consistent. Make a point of keeping your body language and nonverbal cues consistent from interview to interview. It can be exhausting to conduct multiple interviews on the same day or on consecutive days, so guard against letting your nonverbal behaviors creep into successive interviews. Each interviewee deserves an equal chance to be evaluated, and if you allow yourself to let your fatigue or other issues show through, you might miss something important about a particular candidate.

Peer to Peer

Peer-to-peer interactions in the business world can be sources of conflict, information, negotiation, encouragement, or any other of a number of things. Your body language can have a strong influence on the value and outcome of peer-to-peer interactions so it is well worth paying attention to how you come across to the other person. Let's look at these few examples more closely.

Conflict. If you are in conflict with a peer, keep your body language as open and neutral as possible. You don't want to shrink back or appear submissive, but neither do you want to appear too aggressive or dominant. When your nonverbal behaviors are open and accepting, your peer is likely to consciously or unconsciously mirror that behavior. This puts you both in a much better position to resolve the conflict in a constructive rather than destructive way.

Information. Many peer-to-peer interactions are for the purpose of sharing or gathering information. In these situations your body language should encourage the other person to provide information freely. Nodding your head, gestures that communicate "go on, I'm listening," taking notes, and keeping an interested facial expression are all good ways to get the most out of these kinds of interactions.

Negotiation. Negotiation interactions are inherently give and take, sort of like dancing back and forth until you each settle into a comfortable position. Just as with a conflict situation, during negotiation your body language should be open and assertive rather than dominant or submissive. You will have a much harder time coming to agreement if your nonverbal behaviors scream "I'm going to beat you," such as pointing, standing too close, or using a tone of voice that is too forceful.

Encouragement. When someone comes to you needing encouragement, your body language serves as proof of the accuracy of your words. If you are telling that person you care and want to help, but your body language is showing you are impatient and want to get back to what you were doing, your encouragement is not going to be very successful. On the other hand, you can have a very positive effect on that person if you focus your attention, listen closely, keep an open body position, and nod your head along the way.

Manager to Subordinate

Manager-to-subordinate interactions are particularly important because they have the potential for creating so many other ramifications. If you are too aggressive you may be accused of being overbearing; if you are too accommodating you may be accused of being weak. Conversations related to job performance are particularly tough, because you need to clearly communicate the need for improvement while offering encouragement that improvement is within reach.

Because the manager-to-subordinate relationship involves one person having a higher status and more power than the other person, the person with the most power must be the most cautious about using it appropriately. Even the appearance of dominance through aggressive body language can create human resources problems if the subordinate interprets your nonverbal behavior as intimidation or inappropriate use of power.

Whenever possible, conduct these kinds of interactions in the open or at least with the door open. This helps avoid situations where it's your word against the subordinate's word and nobody else witnessed the interaction. Keep your body posture neutral and your gestures relaxed, no matter how animated or energetic the discussion becomes. Remember, you are in the power position literally and figuratively so you have an even greater responsibility to ensure your nonverbal behaviors match your words.

There are times when your subordinate is timid, uncertain, or inexperienced in the business world. When this happens your body language can serve to either help the subordinate gain confidence and experience or to crush what little confidence he already has. Recognize your subordinate's nonverbal cues such as submissive posture, hesitant voice, and difficulty making eye contact. Respond with your own nonverbal cues to build rapport, establish trust, and encourage the person to communicate openly and honestly.

Chapter 8 TAKEAWAYS

1. Body language and nonverbal behaviors are important in the real world of business. They influence how you are perceived, how you are treated, and even the level of success you might achieve.

2. The business environment requires different body language than the personal or private environment. Expectations and perceptions can vary greatly depending on the nature of the business environment. Four common business environments are conservative, casual, industrial, and academic.

3. Your body language during meetings affects how those meetings unfold and the outcomes they produce. Nonverbal cues to consider include where you sit, how you sit, whether or not you sit, how you use your hands, what you bring with you, and how well you adhere to the accepted ground rules.

4. Your body language when selling and your ability to read the body language of your client are important to your sales success. Establish rapport, make an effort to minimize gestures,

choose the appropriate position relative to the other person, and remember to use your voice as a nonverbal tool.

5. Your body language when hiring can affect how the hiring process proceeds as well as the quality of the interviews you conduct. Focus on using an open body position and watch for nonverbal cues from the interviewee to determine if/when additional follow-up questions are in order. Watch for interviewees who are so controlled in their body language that they appear to be covering something up, and be sure that your own body language is consistent from interview to interview.

6. Your body language during peer-to-peer interactions affects the quality and outcomes of those interactions. Some of the most common types of peer-to-peer interactions involve conflict, information exchange, negotiation, and encouragement.

7. Body language is particularly important in manager-to-subordinate interactions because the manager is in a position of greater status and power. Inappropriate nonverbal behaviors can lead to misunderstandings, accusations, or poor mentoring of staff in need of development and support.

Chapter 8 WORKSHEET

---

1. Review the Chapter 8 Takeaways and answer the following:
   - Which key point(s) did you find most interesting? Why?
   - Which key point(s) did you find most surprising? Why?

2. Think about the type of business environment where you work and decide if it is conservative, casual, industrial, or academic. What are the characteristics that caused you to decide on that specific type?

3. Think about the last meeting you attended and the body language of the people who were there. Pick one person and describe his body language in terms of the following:

    Where the person sat.

    How the person sat.

    Whether the person sat.

    The person's hands.

    What the person carried in to the meeting.

    How the person followed the ground rules.

    How did that person's body language affect the conduct and outcome of the meeting? What could the person have done differently to improve either one?

Extra credit: Answer question 3 again, this time focusing on your own body language and nonverbal behaviors.

---

9 | Secret Language of the Sexes

D iscussing differences between the sexes—no matter the topic—is always fun. And in nonverbal communication, men and women are indeed very different.

The fact is there are many differences between the genders in all sorts of areas, including body language and nonverbal behaviors. Body language is one area where distinct differences are readily apparent and actively researched. These differences are fascinating, both in their scope and their purpose for existence.

So as we enter the world of body language and gender, please keep in mind that gender differences are real and serve a purpose within the human condition. This does not mean, however, these differences are automatically better or worse depending on whether they are present in men or women. They are simply differences, not judgments of relative value or overall worth.

The Differences between Men and Women

The differences between men and women occur in behaviors as well as the purpose of those behaviors. They are a wonderful combination of preprogrammed characteristics and culturally learned behaviors, which interact with each other sometimes in very complex ways.

Preprogrammed characteristics are those that serve some sort of basic survival purpose. In men they tend to be related to providing protection, defending territory, and maximizing the passing on of their genes. In women, they tend to be related to attracting a desirable mate, nurturing children, and organizing the social environment.

Culturally learned characteristics, on the other hand, are those that develop in response to environmental and social influences. They tend to differ across cultures and even from generation to generation. In men they tend to be related to masculinity, status, and achieving success. In women, they tend to be related to relationships, connection, and interpersonal aspects of life.

Modern life allows a much greater degree of variability in the development and display of both kinds of nonverbal characteristics. For instance, in the business world many women feel they need to take on traditionally male characteristics of dominance, assertiveness, and power in order to succeed. Many industries and disciplines are still overwhelmingly male, so for women it can truly be a matter of survival to adopt characteristics similar to their male peers. Many other women, however, choose to participate in the business world on their own terms. They deal with so-called male bias by emphasizing their own skills, attributes, and contributions to the business environment. They embrace their dual roles as business professionals and women, blending the two together and making them into one integrated approach to life.

On the other end of the spectrum, modern men are far more likely to feel comfortable letting traditionally female characteristics develop or show through. The acceptability of men expressing emotions, sharing feelings, and nurturing children are more and more evident in today's world and, in fact, are often viewed as highly desirable. Where the traditional male role was to be the breadwinner and head of the family, the modern male role is more often one of partnership, mutual respect, and father. Thirty years ago the idea of a man being a stay-at-home parent was outlandish and considered a joke. Now, however, it is considered a legitimate option for many families and becoming a more frequent choice.

So what does this all mean? The relative freedom to express oneself with authentic body language rather than expected body language has opened up a whole new world of possibilities for men and women alike. Men can display caring, nurturing nonverbal behaviors without putting their masculinity at risk; and women can show assertive, confident body language without abandoning their feminine side.

All of this new freedom is exhilarating, but also creates potential conflict and misunderstanding. For instance, a person might automatically place a hand on a peer's shoulder to express encouragement but the peer might interpret that as an intimate gesture. Or, a person might offer a high five and give a friendly shoulder punch to express happiness but the person on the receiving end might interpret that as a hostile or aggressive behavior.

Self Touch

Women touch themselves more than men . . . a lot more.

You'll notice that I didn't specify male or female in these examples, and I did that for a reason. Men and women are equally capable of demonstrating any of these behaviors, either as the sender or the receiver of nonverbal cues. But think for a moment about how each example might be interpreted differently depending on which gender is in which role. The potential combinations and interpretations are numerous and clearly illustrate the challenge of body language differences between men and women.

Gender Differences in Sending

In general, women are more skilled than men at expressing subtle nonverbal cues. Experts disagree on exactly why this is true, but most agree it has something to do with a woman's preprogrammed characteristics of nurturing and organizing the social environment. Through the use of body language and nonverbal behaviors, a woman can influence others without appearing to do so openly and obviously.

A classic example of this appears in the earliest stages of attraction and courtship. Men usually think they are the initiators when it comes to courtship, but research *shows it is the woman who initiates the process over 90 percent of the time*. How? By using body language and nonverbal cues. For instance, a combination of eye contact, facial expressions, and body movement and positioning sends a powerful signal from the woman to the selected man that she is interested in him and may be open to meeting and getting to know him. He walks across the room, they speak, and the encounter progresses from there. The man thinks he initiated the contact by walking across the room, but in reality the woman initiated the contact by subtly inviting him to make contact.

Gazing
Men tend to not gaze at each other much.
   Men and women both gaze at the opposite sex more.
   Women gaze at other women most!

Another common illustration of gender differences in sending body language messages is the hug. Men tend to hug briefly, firmly, and confidently, while women tend to hug longer, gently, and with more emotion. This is all fine, of course, but think about the misinterpretations that can occur based on these gender differences. Let's say a man hugs a woman to comfort her when she is feeling sad. From her perspective a proper hug is gentle and lasts for several moments, but from his perspective a proper hug is firm and short in duration. So he gives her a hug, thinking he has offered comfort, and she receives that hug, thinking he doesn't really care that much because his hug was so abrupt.

The same sorts of differences appear when men and women speak to another person about personal or emotional issues. A woman will tend to face the other person, lean forward a bit, and use eye contact and facial expressions to communicate her message. A man, on the other hand, will tend to turn sideways or even separate himself from the other person with a bit of distance. He may also choose to communicate his message while doing something, making it seem more of an add-on to the interaction rather than the focus of the interaction.

Of course, there are exceptions to all of these generalizations, and you probably have experiences that differ a little or a lot from the examples I describe. When it comes to real-life interactions, use these examples as general guidelines to help interpret messages being sent but always give greater weight to individual personalities and characteristics.

Smiling

Women smile a little more often than men do.

Women in a room by themselves, smile a lot more than men do when alone.

Women are smiled at a lot more than men are.

Gender Differences in Receiving

It's probably not too surprising that women are generally much better than men at receiving and interpreting body language and nonverbal messages. Research shows very clearly that women are more adept at reading body language, spotting contradictions between verbal and nonverbal messages, and noticing the small details of body language that can reveal so much.

Why do women have these abilities? Experts say it has to do with preprogrammed characteristics designed for child rearing. Infants and toddlers rely almost solely on body language to communicate for the first two years or so, and women as the primary caretakers must be able to read and interpret these messages accurately. This aspect of nature's design can be seen in how men and women differ in the processing of messages inside their brains.

Magnetic Resonance Imaging (MRI) scans of male and female brains reveal a marked difference in how different parts of the brain are used. Women have as many as 16 distinct areas of the brain where they process and interpret the behaviors and messages sent by other people. In contrast, men typically have no more than six distinct areas of the brain where they process and interpret the behaviors and messages sent by other people.

How do these differences show up in real life? Women tend to be better able to multitask and handle several different streams of thought at the same time, while men tend to be better at working through one or two streams of thought at a time before moving on to others. And while women are generally more adept at unconsciously receiving and interpreting nonverbal cues, men are just as capable of reading body language when they learn how to consciously read those signals.

Navigating through the Differences

So what are you to do with this information about gender differences in body language sending and receiving? Use it to approach interactions with gender tendencies in mind as guidelines rather than hard-and-fast rules. They are a starting point only; your real-life interactions will range across the full spectrum of gender differences.

Awareness of gender differences can be very helpful when building rapport, establishing trust, or negotiating differences between genders. When men and women use mirroring body language with each other they build rapport and get a better sense of the other person's perspective and attention to nonverbal cues. In a conflict situation, noticing and appreciating gender differences can make all the difference between resolving a conflict positively or allowing resentment and bitterness to linger.

An obvious place where this approach is beneficial is in a marriage or committed relationship. The close nature of this type of relationship means there must be a great deal of trust and understanding between two people if the relationship is to flourish. A man can benefit by paying attention to the unique body language and nonverbal cues of the woman, as can a woman by paying attention to the unique body language and nonverbal cues of the man. Many a couple has experienced conflict and disagreement when one or the other misinterprets or simply misses altogether important nonverbal cues.

Let's say a man typically arrives home first and takes responsibility for making dinner. One day he gets home particularly tired and frustrated after a very difficult day. His body is slumped, his face is tense, and he's hardly talking or making any eye contact. That same day, the woman arrives home feeling excited and fulfilled after a particularly successful day. She has a bounce in her step, her face is relaxed and smiling, and she is eager to talk and share information. She walks into the kitchen and asks in a bright, cheery tone of voice, "Hi honey, what's for dinner?" Of course you can see the conflict barreling down the tracks in this situation if either the man or the woman does not notice or properly interpret each other's nonverbal cues.

In the business environment, gender differences can lead to dramatically different interpretations of the same set of events. Let's say a man and a woman both attend a meeting where the meeting facilitator acts cold, abrupt, and short tempered. The man is likely to brush this behavior off as not important or judge it to be due to a bad mood. The woman, on the other hand, is likely to pick up on the nonverbal cues sent out by the facilitator. She walks up to the man and comments that the facilitator may be experiencing his recurring back pain and that's why he was so abrupt. The man looks at her blankly, wondering how in the world she came to that conclusion.

The woman probably noticed the facilitator moving stiffly, wincing, or otherwise showing body language that indicated pain and discomfort. She knows the facilitator has an ongoing problem with back pain, so this knowledge combined with her interpretation of his body language leads to her conclusion. The man, on the other hand, probably did not notice the body language of the facilitator. He generates his conclusion based on his own experiences of his behavior when he is in a bad mood.

Can you see how gender differences influenced very different interpretations of the same set of events? How might those different interpretations influence the man's and woman's perceptions of each other? Of the facilitator? What action is each person likely to take next? The woman might choose to speak briefly with the facilitator and inquire about how his back feels, while the man might choose instead to avoid the facilitator for the rest of the day to stay out of the line of fire of his bad mood.

You can see, then, how gender differences influence the sending and receiving of nonverbal messages and how awareness of those differences can help you find your way successfully through a variety of situations. Take a few moments to think about a specific situation in your life where you might put this new awareness to good use, and make a conscious decision to put it into action the next time that situation occurs.

Chapter 9 TAKEAWAYS

1. Gender differences can be difficult to discuss because of long-standing biases and opinions about the nature of those differences. The tendency has almost always been to dismiss women as somehow inferior, but in the modern world this view has changed a great deal.

2. The underlying reasons for gender differences vary and include preprogrammed characteristics as well as culturally influenced characteristics.

3. Men and women differ in their body language and nonverbal behaviors.

4. Men and women differ in the purpose of their body language and nonverbal behaviors.

5. Women are generally more skilled at sending nonverbal messages, most likely due to their preprogrammed characteristics of nurturing children and organizing the social environment.

6. Women are generally more skilled at either consciously or unconsciously receiving nonverbal messages, most likely due in part to differences in how many parts of their brain they use to interpret these messages.

7. Men can become just as skilled at receiving nonverbal messages when they learn how to consciously read those signals.

8. Gender differences in body language and nonverbal behaviors can easily lead to misunderstandings and misinterpretations. They can also be consciously mirrored and interpreted as a way to build rapport and increase understanding.

9. Gender differences in body language show up in the business environment, the home environment, and in relationships and interactions of all kinds. Learning to understand and accommodate these differences can make a big difference in your ability to deal with a variety of situations.

Chapter 9 **WORKSHEET**

---

1. Review the Chapter 9 Takeaways and answer the following:

    ■ Which key point(s) did you find most interesting? Why?
    ■ Which key point(s) did you find most surprising? Why?

2. Identify four different examples of how the modern world allows greater variability in the development and display of nonverbal characteristics:

    Male preprogrammed

    Female preprogrammed

    Male culturally learned

    Female culturally learned

3. Think of a time when gender differences in use and interpretation of body language led to a conflict or disagreement in your life.

    ■ What was your role in the situation?
    ■ What was the other person's role in the situation?

    If you could go back and repeat that situation now with the new knowledge you have about gender differences in nonverbal communication, what would you do differently?

10 | Back Home with the Kids

M any people do not stop to consider the role of body language in parenting, but it is in fact integral to the parental role. Some nonverbal behaviors are exhibited by parents across many different cultures while others are unique and specific to particular cultures.

Parenting guidebooks focus a great deal on techniques and strategies for raising children, but I have yet to find one that incorporates information about body language and nonverbal behaviors as part of the parental tool kit. Remember that for the first two years or so of life, children communicate primarily through body language because they have not yet developed speech and language skills. Even after speech develops, a child communicates a great deal through body language, especially when parents make a point of paying attention to it.

In this chapter, my intent is not to replace other sources of parenting information; after all, I'm an expert on body language, not parenting. Rather, my goal is to extend the study and awareness of body language beyond the classroom and the workplace into the real-life situations people encounter on a regular basis. This kind of linkage between academic information and practical application is what I believe to be most valuable and is an underlying theme of this entire book.

As we move forward on this subject, I encourage you to take a fresh look at how your body language connects with your parenting activities (if you have children, of course). If you do not have children or if you are interested in another perspective, use the information in this chapter to take a fresh look at the way your parents used body language while you were growing up. Chances are you will have an entirely new appreciation for the unconscious (and conscious) effects of nonverbal behaviors in the parent/child relationship.

The Parental Role

I'll begin with a closer look at the parental role itself. You could argue that a parent's job is to do, at a minimum, the following:

- Provide protection, food, and shelter.
- Teach cultural norms and expectations.
- Teach life skills necessary for survival.
- Teach morals, value, and/or spiritual beliefs.
- Prepare a child to become a capable, functional adult.

These are what I consider the very basics of parenting. They take care of a child's physical needs, socialization, rules of behavior, and general survival skills. They do not, however, address the multitude of other aspects of parenting that are just as critical to the development and growth of a child.

Here are a few general categories of parenting I think are important and influenced by the use of body language and nonverbal messages:

- Emotional development.
- Decision-making skills.

■ Goal setting.

■ Work ethic.

■ Social responsibility.

■ Personal responsibility.

Let's take a more detailed look at each of these categories.

Emotional development. This category includes a parent's efforts to help a child learn to better understand and deal with his emotions at different stages of life. A parent might teach about when and where it's appropriate to express anger, enthusiasm, fear, sadness, or any other emotion that might occur. Additionally, a parent is likely to help a child learn to control emotions and understand how they influence other aspects of life.

Decision-making skills. This category is for the lessons a parent teaches about how to evaluate information and make good decisions. A parent might emphasize exploring multiple options, verifying the accuracy of information, or including moral beliefs in the decision-making process. There is a bit of overlap between decision-making skills and emotional development, as emotions can play a powerful role in hasty or unwise decisions.

Goal setting. This category includes a parent's efforts to help a child plan for the future and create long-term growth. A child who doesn't know how to set goals is much like a boat without a rudder, floating about with no clear direction. Commonly encouraged goals might be learning to walk, talk, eat with a spoon, get dressed, tie a pair of tennis shoes, ride a bike, read a book, and so on.

Work ethic. This category is for the ways in which a parent teaches a child about effort and reward, even when that reward is simply the satisfaction of completing a difficult task. It also relates to issues of earning privileges, being responsible, and choosing to do something the right way rather than the easy or convenient way.

Social responsibility. This category includes a parent's guidance about how a child contributes to general society. It might include something as simple as using a garbage can rather than littering, or something more complex like volunteering and doing good works to help improve some aspect of the world, community, or the lives of people. This is the glue that holds cultures together because it ensures each generation will grow up to participate and keep the culture alive, in time passing that same sense of social responsibility on to their own offspring.

Personal responsibility. This category is for the influence of a parent on a child's development of accountability and understanding of the relationship between actions and consequences. It may show up as warning a small child not to throw toys and putting the child in time-out for throwing a toy after having been warned. This pattern of requiring accountability and enforcing the connection between actions and consequences is one way in which a parent instills a sense of personal responsibility in a child.

Now, I said earlier that I'm not a parenting expert, I'm a body language expert, so you might wonder why I'm including all of these areas of focus that relate to how a parent raises a child. The connection here is that these are all common areas addressed by parents and parents commonly use body language and nonverbal behaviors to teach or reinforce these concepts.

Here is that list of parenting categories again, but this time with examples of how nonverbal communication is part of the overall teaching process:

Emotional development. Facial expressions are important for teaching and modeling emotional development lessons, such as when a parent smiles at a child who uses words to express anger rather than hitting. Nodding or shaking the head is another way a parent communicates whether a child is handling emotions appropriately or emphasizes key points when having a discussion with the child.

Decision-making skills. A parent might use exaggerated body language to teach about decision-making skills related to selecting an appropriate toy for a particular circumstance. If it is play time, for instance, movements that imitate throwing a ball or riding a bike might be used to help a child choose whether to go outdoors or sit in front of the TV. If it is nearing bedtime, however, hugging a teddy bear and putting away a race car helps a child decide on a more calming toy that will help him settle down for the night.

Goal setting. Parents use a lot of body language to encourage and reward goal setting. For instance, when an infant is first learning to walk, a parent will use facial expressions, gestures, and body movement to encourage the child to give it a try and reward the child for the effort even if he doesn't succeed. Every time the parent smiles and claps for the baby who is trying to walk, the message the child receives is, "You can do it, keep challenging yourself and you can learn to walk."

Work ethic. A parent who assigns a child to rake the leaves will reinforce the importance of working diligently in several ways. The parent might work alongside the child doing a similar task or make a point of checking on progress and offering a pat on the back for continued effort. The message received by the child is that it is important to keep working and complete the task, even if the task is unpleasant or there is something more enjoyable the child could be doing at that moment.

Social responsibility. A parent who walks past litter, drops a piece of garbage, or pretends not to see a garbage can is sending powerful nonverbal messages about the importance of throwing garbage away in a proper receptacle. The message is that it doesn't matter if the child litters or not, even if the parent's words say the child should use a garbage can. The nonverbal message conflicts with the verbal message and has greater influence than the verbal message.

Personal responsibility. A parent might enforce the lesson of personal responsibility by deliberately avoiding eye contact with a child who is screaming and upset about being put in time-out. The message is that the consequence remains in effect whether the child likes it or not, so in the future the child should be more accountable for the actions he chooses to take.

That's enough of body language and its relationship to parenting in general. Let's move on to body language and nonverbal behaviors and how they influence interactions with children of different ages.

Newborns and Infants

Newborns and infants are preprogrammed to respond to body language, most especially facial expressions. They quickly learn to recognize the happy, smiling face of a parent and work mightily to learn how to smile back. Newborns use body language of their own to communicate with their parents, such as making a sucking motion when hungry or scrunching up the legs when stomach gas is causing pain. The parent interprets these nonverbal messages and takes action to provide whatever it is the newborn needs.

As infants grow and learn to crawl around, their use of and understanding of body language continues to grow as well. For example, if the infant reaches for something fragile and off limits such as a vase, the parent uses a stern tone of voice to say no, scrunches up the face to show disapproval, and shakes the head back and forth to further send the message that the child should leave the vase alone. Infants will also use their own body language to check in with their parents if they are in doubt about whether something is allowed or not. Take that same vase sitting on a coffee table. The child might edge closer and closer to the vase, periodically looking back at the parent for a sign of approval or disapproval. The child might even reach out and attempt to touch the vase, again looking to the parent for some signal indicating whether they are allowed to do that.

A parent's body language is part of teaching an infant how to begin eating soft baby foods. The parent takes a small spoonful of baby food and opens his mouth as the spoon moves closer to the baby's mouth. The parent's open mouth is a nonverbal signal encouraging the baby to imitate that same behavior. Once the food is in the baby's mouth the parent might make chewing and swallowing motions, again encouraging the baby to imitate that behavior. And of course, there is always the technique of the parent eating a spoonful of baby food and smiling happily (no matter how bad it tastes) to encourage the baby to try a spoonful, too.

Toddlers and Preschoolers

Toddlers and preschoolers are mobile and can move quickly. Their impulsiveness often leads to actions and behaviors that are unacceptable or even dangerous, such as running into a parking lot, hitting another child, or pulling a dog's tail. A parent's body language then becomes important for showing approval and disapproval as well as guiding the child's movements in the desired direction and at the desired speed.

A very important word for a parent to teach a child is "stop" because it instantly communicates an important message to the child. Body language—such as a stern tone of voice, a stern facial expression, or a hand gesture with palm forward in a signal to stop—is part of that teaching process. The more the parent uses this combination of nonverbal cues, the quicker the child learns what they mean. Many toddlers get to the point where simply giving the hand gesture to stop is enough to get their attention and keep them from doing something they shouldn't.

The issue of running into the parking lot is another one that can be addressed very well with a combination of verbal and nonverbal cues. While the parent tells the child to stop at the curb, take his hand,

and look both ways, the parent uses body language to communicate the same messages. A hand gesture indicates the child should stop, an outstretched hand indicates the child should grab hold of the hand, and exaggerated motions of looking both ways teaches the child exactly what look both ways really means.

Preschoolers are especially good at picking up on nonverbal messages from a parent when they are learning a new activity or skill. For example, the proper use of a paint brush becomes more clear when the parent demonstrates or imitates dipping the brush in paint, wiping the excess on the edge of the cup, and smoothing the paint onto the paper.

Sometimes, though, a preschooler's ability to learn from body language leads to unintended consequences, such as when a parent is talking on the phone and makes a talking motion with the hand to indicate the person on the phone is rambling on and on. The next time the child thinks the parent or another child is rambling on too long he is likely to make that same hand motion. Then you get to explain to the child why it was okay for the parent to use that motion but not okay for the child to use that motion.

School-age

School-age children learn a great deal from a parent's body language, too. Learning to shoot a basketball, for example, the parent might use hand and body motion to indicate the correct technique and motion for the child to imitate.

School-age children start to explore the world around them in earnest and embrace perceived expectations for their gender. A parent's nonverbal cues can influence both of these activities. For instance, the parent might use body language to teach a child the proper way to use a shovel to dig holes and look for worms. The parent demonstrates how to hold the shovel, how to loosen the ground, and often pantomimes along as the child gives it a try.

Also, a parent can dispel or reinforce gender expectations through conscious or unconscious body language. A parent whose little boy picks up a worm is likely to act interested and ask the boy to show what he found. But if that same parent has a little girl who picks up a worm, the first impulse might be to make a yucky face, make a negative sound, and use an arm gesture to encourage the girl to put the worm down right away. What is the clear message communicated to each child in this situation? It's okay for boys to be interested in worms, it's not okay for girls to be interested in worms.

A growing number of parents deserve a lot of credit, though, for being aware of how their body language influences gender choices and expectations. Nowadays it is common for parents to be just as interested when a girl picks up a worm as when a boy does the same thing. Girls are receiving more and more nonverbal cues that it's okay to be assertive, to try new things, to be good at math and science, to pursue their dreams, and so on. In the same vein, boys are receiving more and more nonverbal cues that it's okay to be compassionate, to be nurturing, to compromise, and to be friends with girls as well as boys.

The next time you see a parent with a school-age child, observe their interactions, and look for body language messages between the parent and child. See how the parent consciously or unconsciously communicates with the child and influences the child's actions or behaviors.

Preteen

The preteen years are sort of like a preview of what's to come, much like a movie trailer shows you a bit about a film that's coming soon to your local theater. There is just enough information in that trailer to give you a glimpse into the film but not enough to reveal to you the entire story. Interacting with a preteen is nearly the same; you catch a glimpse of what might be on the way during the teen years but you can't yet take in the entire story.

Preteens are also experiencing the first changes in their bodies that eventually lead to puberty. Boys start to notice girls, girls start to notice boys, and parents start to notice subtle changes in their relationship with opposite gender children. A preteen girl who used to gleefully jump on her father and pretend to wrestle him to the ground might suddenly stop doing that and even be reluctant to hug or be hugged by her father. The father might ask the girl what is wrong, but the girl doesn't really know, either. All she knows is she doesn't want her father to hug her. Fathers who see these kinds of changes need to pay close attention to the nonverbal cues their daughters are sending and be respectful of their growing need for privacy and less physical contact with their fathers.

Boys often show behavior that is similar but has some slightly different nuances. For instance, the mother who used to give her son a kiss and hug good-bye before school may suddenly find her son physically resisting or protesting that formerly welcomed hug and kiss. He's likely to just wave and say good-bye or perhaps not even wave at all as he goes out the door to school.

However, it is not at all unusual for preteen boys to still crave their mother's hugs deep down inside. They just don't want to admit it because they are facing pressures to grow up and stop being a little boy. Every once in a while, though, when nobody else is around and the boy has a moment of quiet time with his mother, he'll wrap his arms around her and squeeze her tight, of course receiving a hug that is just as emotional in return. It may only last a moment or two, but in that brief time span the body language between mother and son is unmistakable. Affection, love, appreciation, and security are just a few of the messages going back and forth between them. Just as suddenly as it started it ends, and the boy wanders away again, but the nonverbal communication continues to have a powerful impact.

I mentioned earlier that preteen boys and girls start to notice each other more, and there is a parental influence on this phenomenon as well. Parents who are open and accessible to their children are much better able to communicate with their children during this time of conflicting emotions. The parents who welcome their daughter's first crush when he comes over after school and treat him as a legitimate part of her life set the stage for future years when her relationships become longer and more serious. She will be more likely to bring her boyfriends home and feel comfortable just hanging out there, which is great from the parent's standpoint because it's much easier to keep tabs on exactly what she is doing.

Remember that the preteen years may be just as confusing for parents as they are for children, because nobody is entirely comfortable with the changing feelings and emotions. The best way to get through this phase and on to the real teenage years is to be extra conscious of body language, both yours and your child's, and be open to the messages being communicated.

Teen and Young Adult

As soon as parents get through the preteen phase, next up are the teen and young adult years. This is perhaps the most tumultuous time in a parent/child relationship and one that can go on for only a couple of years or extend out further over many years. As difficult as it may be sometimes, maintaining connection and communication is critical to parents and teens successfully navigating their way through this time, and body language can be an extremely revealing communication tool.

Teens have this amazing ability to push you away at the same time they want you to stay near, both literally and figuratively. Modern brain scan research has revealed that the teenage brain undergoes a huge burst of development, which contributes to a teen's notorious tendency toward mood swings, strong emotions, and an apparent lack of impulse control or common sense. The good news is that this kind of behavior is entirely normal, and it presents unique opportunities for parents to connect with their teens.

Parents can tell a lot about a teen by paying attention to body language. It is usually not too difficult to detect the subtle signs of stress, worry, anger, or sadness; what is difficult is getting the teen to open up and talk about those feelings. Even as a teen attempts to push parents away, there are often subtle nonverbal messages that are screaming for the parents to be persistent and stick with their teen. For instance, if a teen's behavior takes a sudden, unusual turn, or if activities that used to bring enjoyment are now abandoned or ignored, it's a good bet the parents need to open up communication and give some support and/or guidance to their child.

Young adults, especially those who are college age, require a different style of parenting altogether. They are truly beginning to venture out on their own, and parents walk a very fine line between letting them go and maintaining a bit of gentle guidance. Parents can use body language as a powerful communication tool for letting their young adult children know they are appreciated and respected as emerging adults. Be open and accessible, but don't hover or hang around too much. Set up house rules to govern issues such as laundry, curfew, food, privacy, and chores. It is not unreasonable to expect a young adult living at home to contribute a bit of rent or take on a specific set of chores in lieu of rent. The parents' verbal and nonverbal communication must be consistent in this situation, establishing rules and holding the young adult accountable for following them.

Adult Children

The relationship between parents and their adult children can cover an entire range of possibilities, from close and personal to distant or nonexistent. Often adult children go through a period of time where they consciously avoid interacting with their parents too much as a way of asserting and demonstrating their own independence. This can be very hard on parents, but the right balance of connection and freedom can lead to a closer relationship later on.

What is that right balance? It differs for everyone, of course, but body language and nonverbal behaviors can give you a pretty good idea of where that balance lies. Keep your body language open, friendly, and caring, but not overwhelming or smothering. Recognize that your adult children may not feel as comfortable hugging you as they did when they were children, and if they have a spouse or partner that person may not be comfortable with hugs, either. It's okay to reach out to adult children, but watch for signs that they feel you are getting too close or too personal. As much as you would like to be a close confidante, chances are your adult children prefer someone else to fulfill that role. The more accepting and understanding you are of their wishes, both spoken and unspoken, the better your relationship is likely to be over the long term.

Grandchildren

Everything changes when grandchildren come along. Suddenly your baby has a baby of his own, and you are not the primary decision maker on parenting issues. Thankfully, you get to fulfill an even more rewarding role—grandparent. This is a very special and privileged position, providing a multitude of opportunities for sharing, caring, laughter, and love.

One of the best things you can do for your grandchildren is to love them unconditionally and indulge them a little bit. Not too much, of course, because you certainly don't want them to end up spoiled, but just enough so that time spent with you is a treat and a welcome break from the routine of everyday life.

Body language fits into this relationship quite nicely. A broad smile and welcoming facial expression lets your grandchildren know they are the focus of your attention and a source of great pride. Wide open arms, ready to give a special hug or a playful swing up into the air, also communicate that you love and value your grandchildren.

When you have grandchildren, you have a wonderful opportunity to enjoy the wonders of childhood without the huge responsibility of being the parent. You can get down on the floor and play blocks, because laundry can wait until your grandchild heads home. This kind of focused attention and close participation clearly communicates that your grandchild is important to you and worthy of your attention.

Many grandparents develop special signals or gestures with their grandchildren, something silly or sweet or simple that is shared between grandparent and grandchild. For instance, you might blow a kiss to your grandchildren as they leave your house to head home. Or, you might have a special bear hug or even a handshake for when you greet them or say good-bye to them. Even if it seems silly to you, remember that these little signs are huge and important from a grandchild's perspective. They are anchor points and rituals that reassure your grandchildren of your role in their lives. Years and years down the road, you may even find your grandchildren still remember those nonverbal signals and want to continue using them because they have such a powerful meaning and connection.

In today's world of blended families, it's very possible you could end up with new step grandchildren at some point. In these situations you need to be extra vigilant about body language and nonverbal cues, because the new members of your family may not know quite what to expect. They may have had very different experiences when they were little, or be struggling with the adjustment of living within a stepfamily. The best approach is usually to be friendly, welcoming, and open with your body language, and don't push yourself onto the new grandchildren. Let them become comfortable with you; don't worry, you know a lot about body language so you'll see the nonverbal cues.

And here's something else to consider. In blended families, grandparents can play an important role in helping the new family members grow closer together. Share a favorite story of something your adult child did when he or she was younger, and your new step grandchildren just might feel a bit better about their new family.

The most important thing to remember about body language and grandchildren is that they really do pick up on your nonverbal messages. It's often unconscious and they may not fully understand how they are able to receive the messages, but they do understand the meaning and importance of those messages. Give your grandchildren the focus, respect, and unconditional love they deserve, and you will reap the rewards throughout their lives.

Chapter 10 TAKEAWAYS

1. Body language and nonverbal behaviors are powerful but often overlooked tools of parenting. Babies spend the first two years or so communicating exclusively through body language, so they are attuned to nonverbal messages right from the very beginning.

2. Parents have the basic role of providing the necessities of life, but they also have the broader role of guiding their children through emotional development, learning decision-making skills, goal setting, developing a work ethic, and embracing social responsibility and personal responsibility.

3. Body language and nonverbal behaviors play a role in all of these important parental roles, ranging from facial expressions to body movements to gestures to modeling behaviors.

4. Newborns and infants respond especially to facial expressions, and as they grow will actively look to parents for nonverbal cues of approval or disapproval.

5. Body language can help regulate and guide the movements and behaviors of toddlers and preschoolers. Consistent use of body language such as a hand gesture to stop or demonstrating how to use a paint brush can help a young child understand more clearly what is expected.

6. School-age children are sensitive to body language and non-verbal messages, especially those related to gender expectations. Parents can literally shape a girl's or boy's perspective of gender roles through conscious use of body language and nonverbal behaviors.

7. Preteens are at the very beginning of tremendous changes in their bodies, which often leads to changes in their body language and nonverbal behaviors. What's more, they often become uncomfortable and try to distance themselves from their opposite gender parent. This phase is a good time to practice nonverbal communication skills in preparation for the more turbulent teen and young adult years.

8. Teens and young adults are going through physical as well as emotional changes. Parents can help their kids through this phase by paying close attention to their body language and keep the lines of communication connected.

9. Adult children may distance themselves from parents as they go out and establish themselves as adults. Good communication and allowing them their space often leads to closer relationships later on.

10. Grandchildren represent a communication and interaction opportunity like you have never had before. Show them open, loving body language and you will develop rich, rewarding relationships with them.

Chapter 10 WORKSHEET

1. Review the Chapter 10 Takeaways and answer the following:
   ■ Which key point(s) did you find most interesting? Why?
   ■ Which key point(s) did you find most surprising? Why?

2. Think about a time when the body language and nonverbal behaviors of your parents had an effect on you.
   ■ What messages were you receiving?
   ■ How did you respond?
   ■ What could they have done differently?

3. Now think about a time when your body language and nonverbal behaviors had an effect on your own children.
   ■ What messages were you sending?
   ■ How did they respond?
   ■ What could you have done differently?

4. If your children are old enough, start a discussion about what they remember about interactions with you.
   ■ How did they know when you were in a good mood?
   ■ How did they know when you were in a bad mood?

11

Using The Secret Language of Business

So far in this book I've talked quite a bit about practical applications of body language and nonverbal behaviors, mostly in terms of how to recognize nonverbal cues in different situations and just a touch on how to adapt your own body language to those situations. In this chapter I'll focus solely on how to actively use body language to your benefit in various circumstances.

Active use of body language is just one way to improve your overall communication skills, but it comes with some extra responsibility. Most other people do not have the same knowledge or awareness you are developing through this book, so you in essence have a communication advantage. It is important to use that advantage appropriately and not to take advantage of another person. I'll discuss this in more detail in the last section of the chapter.

Body Language in the Real World

By this point, I hope you have a clear understanding of perhaps the most important underlying truth about body language—it affects everything we say, do, think, and feel. Most of the time this influence is unconscious and automatic so you probably have no idea it is even occurring.

Even with the knowledge gained here, you have only just begun to scratch the surface of the power of body language. It is deeply ingrained in the human experience and some might argue it actually defines the human experience. Philosophical discussions aside, body language is an inescapable part of the real world so it makes perfect sense to study it. You can apply what you learn to your relationships, your casual interactions, even your own self talk.

Most people are surprised when I mention applying nonverbal communication skills to self talk because they think in terms of interacting with other people not themselves. But who is the one person with whom you have the most constant and most intimate interactions? Yourself, that's who, and you can have a powerful influence on your inner thoughts through the use of body language.

For instance, the next time you feel irritable, force yourself to smile and walk with a bit of a bounce in your step. If you do this for a short period of time you will actually start to feel a bit better. Another example is when you are walking down the street in an unfamiliar area and you are not sure which direction to go. If you walk with your shoulders slumped and head hanging down you'll feel nervous, uncomfortable, and unsure. But if you walk with your shoulders back and your head up in a confident manner, you'll start to feel more confident and comfortable.

The concept of mind and body influencing beliefs and feelings is called neuro-linguistic programming (NLP) and although the scientific research is somewhat mixed, in practice NLP is often effective for changing thought patterns and behavior patterns. Of course NLP is more complex than just this brief description, but since it is not the primary focus of this book I'll not delve into it any further. Instead, I'll turn to the two areas most often associated with the study of body language.

The two most-searched terms related to body language are "liking," usually in the context of flirting and sexual attraction, and "deception," which makes perfect sense because those are the two things you most often ask yourself before, during, and after an interaction. For instance, you might think:

- Did he/she like me?

- Was he/she telling me the truth?

- Was he/she trying to deceive me?

- Could he/she tell how much I like him/her?

- Did it look like I was telling the truth?

- Do you think the new vendor rep was telling us the truth?

- Could you tell how much I dislike him/her?

- Did he/she get the message that I don't want to see him/her anymore?

- Did the interviewer like me?

- Should I believe it when my boss says there won't be any layoffs?

In other words, in nearly every interaction you have there is an element of like/dislike and truth/deception, and these are the exact elements that body language and nonverbal behaviors convey most clearly. When it comes to using body language to your benefit, then, your best bet is to use it as a way to help answer those questions related to liking and deception.

For the sake of simplicity, I'll devote the remainder of this chapter to four main aspects of liking and deception:

1.   Communicating like/dislike.

2.   Receiving like/dislike.

3.   Communicating truth/deception.

4.   Receiving truth/deception.

All four of these actions can occur in many different situations, such as selling, negotiating, job interviews, friendship, romance, first impressions, business transactions, and much more. That's why I chose them—they all have very strong and very useful practical applications.

Sending Powerful Nonverbal Messages in the Real World

You already use nonverbal communication constantly; it's just your awareness of it that is changing. With this greater awareness, then, you can make conscious decisions about your body language to help you communicate more clearly and more effectively in nearly any situation.

Communicating Like/Dislike

You form an opinion about every single encounter you have, whether you are interacting directly, indirectly, or just passing by, and your body language communicates that opinion. Your opinion might be about a person, a topic of conversation, an event or activity, or something you observe.

Here are some examples of body language you might exhibit (consciously or unconsciously) to communicate like or dislike in various circumstances:

Like at work—Active eye contact, genuine smile and happy facial expression, nod your head, hand gesture greeting, turn toward the person, lean forward, head up, shoulders back, arms in relaxed position, pat on the back, listen intently, move or stand closer, mirroring.

Dislike at work—Minimum eye contact and only when required, neutral facial expression or brief polite smile, turn away from the person, head held still or shaking back and forth, shoulders and head slightly down as if trying to move away or avoid being seen, shift weight back and forth, step back, walk away, hand gesture with palm forward to stop or halt.

Like at a concert—Rapt attention to the performer, lean forward, smile, applause, nodding head or moving body in time to music, humming with music.

Dislike at a concert—Looking around the venue, staring off into space, daydreaming, slump back in seat, flip through program, elbow on arm of chair and head tilted into palm of hand, turn sideways or slightly away from performer, weak or no applause.

Like in a public place—Brief eye contact, brief smile or nod of head, confident walk without changing direction, shoulders back, arms relaxed or swinging slightly.

Dislike in a public place—Avoid eye contact, turn face or head slightly away, change walking direction to create more distance, turn back slightly away when passing, neutral facial expression or slight sneer.

Like on a date—Frequent and direct eye contact; smile and animated facial expressions; lean forward; brief touches of hand, arm, or shoulder; relaxed hand gestures; active listening; walk and sit at close distance.

Dislike on a date—Minimum eye contact, polite smile and neutral facial expressions, shoulders slightly slumped, lean back, look away frequently, few hand gestures, passive or polite listening, walk and sit at greater distance, avoid or pull back from touching.

Want to Communicate a Sense of Genuine Liking?
Don't smile as much as you are inclined to.

Then, when you want to show someone you really like him you can send a much more believable, real smile.

This kind of contrast makes for a potent message.

Communicating Truth/Deception

When you speak, your words convey varying degrees of truth. This does not necessarily mean you deliberately lie (although that does happen) but rather that you don't always say with 100 percent honesty what you really think, feel, or know.

Here are some examples of body language you might exhibit (consciously or unconsciously) to communicate truth or deception in various circumstances:

Truth when you like a coworker's outfit—Smile broadly, open eyes wide, raise eyebrows, say ooh and ahhh, clap hands once or twice, thumbs up, nod head, hand gesture to twirl around, lean forward, move closer.

Deception when you don't like a coworker's outfit—Polite smile, brief smile, nod head slightly.

Truth when client asks about an order—Direct eye contact, lean forward, reassuring hand gesture, neutral facial expression or slight smile, turn slightly sideways and lean in to show client the shipping manifest.

Deception when planning a surprise party—Direct but brief eye contact, smile and tilt head, shake head in denial, turn away to end conversation, nonchalant walk into the party location.

Truth about personal feelings—Direct eye contact; sit facing and at close distance; lean forward; touch hand, arm, or knee; neutral facial expression or smiling expression; minimal hand gestures.

Deception about why you are leaving the CEO's picnic early—Brief eye contact, neutral to apologetic facial expression, shoulder shrug with palms up hand gesture, lean back slightly, move toward the exit.

Truth about a negative performance review—Calm and even tone of voice, neutral body position, steady eye contact, incidental hand gestures, nod and/or shake head.

Deception when unexpected guests drop in—Forced smile, pleasant facial expression, briefly shake hands, sit down toward front of the chair, upright and slightly stiff posture, hands clasped together with elbows resting on the chair or your knees, move toward door to encourage them to leave.

Receiving Nonverbal Messages in the Real World

The body language and nonverbal messages you receive from other people are powerful guideposts during an interaction. They let you know if your messages are meeting with approval or disapproval, regardless of the topic of the message. This allows you to adjust or tailor the communication to address dislikes and emphasize likes, either during the interaction or at a later time.

Receiving Like/Dislike

Just as you form opinions about people, events, topics of conversation, and the like, other people form opinions as well. They communicate their approval or disapproval in the same ways you do, but if you are aware of their body language and nonverbal behaviors it is easier for you to navigate through the conversation and achieve a desired outcome.

Here are some examples of how you might respond when others exhibit (consciously or unconsciously) body language communicating their like or dislike in various circumstances:

Like the car you have for sale—Smile with a positive facial expression, nod your head, use a hand gesture toward something they like about the car, keep steady eye contact, alternately lean slightly forward toward the person then toward the car, step back and give some distance to allow person to consult with another person.

Dislike your opinion about a topic—Steady eye contact, neutral body posture, neutral facial expression, slight head tilt to indicate you're listening, hand gestures to emphasize key points when you respond, stand steady without stepping forward aggressively or back submissively.

Like your budget proposal—Pleasant but not overly excited facial expression, lean slightly forward, reassuring hand gestures, nod your head, steady eye contact.

Dislike the anniversary gift you bought—Listen attentively; hand gesture to touch hand, arm, or shoulder; lower your chin and nod slightly to show regret; move closer and make steady eye contact; calm tone of voice; sincere facial expression.

Like you during a job interview—Lean slightly forward, emphasize well-received statements with mild hand gestures, relax body posture slightly but not too much, mirror the interviewer's body language, smile, steady eye contact.

Dislike the quality of service you provided—Neutral facial expression, listen attentively and nod head occasionally, calm tone of voice, mild hand gestures, slight palms up and hands outward movement.

Like your romantic advances—Smile; lean forward; sit or stand closer; touch of the hand, arm, shoulder, or cheek; steady eye contact; nod your head.

Dislike your speech or presentation—Relax body posture a bit, shift tone of voice to conversational, make eye contact, step toward audience, smile slightly with a positive facial expression.

Receiving Truth / Deception

When others communicate they express varying degrees of truth, just as you do, and they are not necessarily lying deliberately, just as is the case with you. When you are aware of their body language and nonverbal behaviors you are better able to evaluate the level of truth or deception and respond accordingly.

Here are some examples of how you might respond when others exhibit (consciously or unconsciously) body language communicating truth or deception in various circumstances:

> *Truth about ending a relationship*—Sit or stand at a slightly greater distance than usual, maintain an open posture, listen attentively, steady eye contact, neutral facial expression.

> *Deception when you ask for a raise*—Steady eye contact, calm tone of voice, maintain steady distance, neutral body posture, listen attentively to answers given to your questions, medium hand gestures to emphasize your words, calm and steady walk out of the room or office.

> *Truth about why your daughter missed curfew*—Steady and direct eye contact, neutral facial expression, firm and authoritative body posture, calm tone of voice, reassuring hand gesture or touch.

> *Deception about why client purchased from someone else*—Neutral facial expression, calm hand gestures to emphasize key points, steady eye contact, friendly to neutral tone of voice, normal handshake, confident walk, upright body posture.

> *Truth about a poor quality financial report*—Open body posture, steady eye contact, nod to affirm true statements, slight lean forward to show attentiveness, calm tone of voice, minimal hand gestures.

Deception about the taste of a special meal—Smile and pleasant facial expression, maintain eye contact, head up and shoulders in neutral position, relaxed hand gestures, listen attentively, pleasant tone of voice.

Observing Nonverbal Messages in the Real World

When you observe nonverbal communication in the real world, it is rarely as simple and straightforward as the examples I have used throughout this book. The fact is that during any interaction, the body language and nonverbal behaviors of all participants are constantly in motion, changing and adapting and responding to each other. It is this very dynamic nature of nonverbal communication that makes it so powerful, because you can use it to navigate through the natural ebb and flow of an interaction.

A great way to sharpen your understanding of body language and nonverbal behavior is to consciously observe the interactions all around you. This does not mean staring at people and scribbling notes about their every movement and nuance, but it does mean paying attention to the body language of others and practicing to improve your ability to read that body language.

For instance, the next time you are in a staff meeting and the group leader singles out someone for praise, watch how the leader uses body language to reinforce the verbal message and watch how the recipient responds. What can you learn from the exchange? Is there something you can adapt for your own use when you are recognizing and praising your own employees?

Volunteer to help in your child's classroom and observe how the teacher uses the students' body language to help guide her instruction. Are the kids fidgeting in their chairs a bit because they have been sitting down for a long stretch of time? Watch how the teacher pauses to have everyone stand up, stretch, shake their arms and legs, and make a funny face before sitting back down again. Chances are the class has stopped fidgeting and she can move along with the lesson because the kids are paying attention to her again. What can you learn from this? Can you take a cue from the teacher and use awareness of your child's body language as part of your parenting in the home environment?

Remember that you can learn a lot about what not to do when observing others as well. For instance, the cashier at the grocery store looks at the long line of customers waiting in line and rolls her eyes, shakes her head, and turns back to her regular pace of ringing up groceries. How do the people in line respond to her obvious negative attitude about the amount of work ahead of her? Does her body language influence them to be more patient about waiting in line or less patient about waiting in line? Do you see anything of yourself in her reaction? If so, what will you do differently in the future?

If you work in any type of sales position then you are probably already very attuned to body language and nonverbal behavior because it helps you interact more successfully with customers and make more sales. But what if you don't work in sales? What if your job is in a cubicle somewhere, surrounded by row after row of other cubicles with people just like you focused on doing their jobs?

Awareness of body language can still help you a great deal, in terms of maintaining pleasant relationships with others around you, recognizing and meeting behavioral expectations, and such. You'll know right away if you've gone overboard with the Christmas lights in your cubicle or if others appreciate the festive decorations.

Anytime you are interviewing for a new job, observing the body language of the interviewers and especially of other workers if you have the chance to see the work area can tell you a lot about the work atmosphere at that employer. Do you see employees smiling, walking with a bounce in their step, saying hello in the hallways, or working closely in teams? Or do you see employees with their heads down, no eye contact, no conversation, and backs turned to each other? This is very powerful information to notice and can be a great help in deciding if a particular employer is a good fit for your personality and work style. It is especially powerful if the interviewer describes the workplace atmosphere as something very different from what you observe, because your observations are probably the more accurate picture of what it is like to work there.

Is It Influence or Manipulation?

At the very beginning of this chapter I touched on the issue of how your awareness of body language and nonverbal behavior gives you a communication advantage in an interaction. With that extra advantage comes an extra responsibility to use it appropriately.

What does it mean when I say "use it appropriately?" It means you must understand the difference between using nonverbal cues to influence communication and using nonverbal cues to manipulate communication. It is perfectly appropriate to influence a conversation if you are trying to persuade a client to make a purchase, reassure a child he is loved and appreciated, or reinforce a statement you make to an audience.

It is not appropriate, however, to use body language in a way that manipulates others into doing, saying, thinking, or agreeing to something that you know is not in their best interest or is dishonest. For instance, let's say you and a colleague have opposite opinions on the best way to deal with a manufacturing problem. The boss has called a meeting to discuss the situation, so before the meeting starts you pay a visit to your colleague. You use an aggressive tone of voice, a dominating body posture, and threatening hand gestures to tell your colleague he should defer to your opinion and not even mention his opinion in the meeting.

That's manipulation. And it's wrong (and stupid).

But what if the nonverbal cues you use are not as clear cut as what I've described? What if a body movement you perceive as assertive is perceived as threatening by another person? Were you using nonverbal behavior to influence or to manipulate? The answer, of course, will differ depending on whether it comes from you or from the other person.

There is a lot of room for nuance and interpretation when it comes to influence and manipulation, but the truth usually comes down to two very basic issues: integrity and intent.

Integrity and Intent

When a nonverbal behavior occurs in that grey area between influence and manipulation, the truth of the matter is based on the integrity and the intent of the behavior. In other words, was the body language used with a positive intent or a negative intent? Did it occur with integrity or with a disingenuous thought process? These are somewhat murky concepts to grasp, but they get to the very heart of my earlier statements about using the power of body language in an appropriate way. You know, way down deep inside of you, whether you are approaching an interaction with integrity and positive intent.

Here's an example of what I mean. You have most likely seen fortune tellers at carnivals and fairs who claim to have the power to read your energy and see into your future. They charge money for you to have the privilege of sitting down in their tent or trailer to hear what they have to say about you and the path your life will take. The reality is that a fortune teller does not have ESP (shock!) or a mystical ability to see into the future; she is simply very good at reading body language and nonverbal cues.

The sitting usually starts out with some general statement about your life so far, perhaps mentioning you have experienced disappointments along the way and that there are things you want to change in the future. This is of course a very general statement that is probably true for 100 percent of the people who sit down in that room, but it is delivered with such drama and focus on you that you believe the fortune teller knows things about you that she could only discover through a mystical talent. Your body language reflects your feelings and the fortune teller moves forward from there, taking cues from your nonverbal behaviors.

Now, some fortune tellers accept as true that they have a gift and a special talent and that they are doing you a huge favor by providing you with fortune telling services. These people approach the interaction with a degree of integrity and positive intent because they truly believe their abilities are extraordinary. Unfortunately, though, many fortune tellers know full well they do not have a mystical gift. They deliberately manipulate you into paying for their services and consciously read your body language and nonverbal cues as they talk. These are the people who approach the interaction with disingenuous thoughts and a negative intent, because they know their so-called gifts are not real.

Lots of other people cross the line from influence to manipulation, too, such as:

- The used car salesperson who stands in front of a small dent in the fender so you can't see it.
- The adult who emotionally or physically abuses a child.
- The sales clerk who says, "This is the last one," to push you into making a purchase, only to pull another one out of the drawer after you leave.
- The spiritual leader who uses faith and position to solicit your financial donations.
- The spouse who walks out every time there is a disagreement so that you will give in and avoid conflict.

- The schoolyard bully who demands lunch money from the new kid.

- The advertising agency that creates an ad making something sound like a great bargain, only to hide in the fine print that it isn't such a great bargain after all.

The list of possible examples goes on and on and on.

If you are tempted to misuse the knowledge you have gained about body language and nonverbal behavior, remember this: You may get away with it once, twice, or even more times, but eventually others will catch on to what you are doing and then you will have to deal with the consequences. You might lose customers, you might lose influence, you might lose the respect of someone who is important to you, or you might experience a consequence that is totally different from these examples. But rest assured there will be consequences and chances are you will not like them.

I sound a bit like Obi-Wan Kenobi warning Luke Skywalker to beware of the dark side in Star Wars, don't I? There is a very positive aspect to this whole discussion, and I'll close the chapter from this more upbeat perspective.

Your knowledge of body language and nonverbal behavior puts you in an excellent position to avoid the kind of manipulation I have described here. What's more, you can share that knowledge with others so they can reap a similar benefit as well. I encourage you to go forward with your new awareness and do your part to be a positive influence on others.

Chapter 11 TAKEAWAYS

1. The study and awareness of body language has many practical applications in the real world. It allows you to better interpret and understand interactions and improve the quality and effectiveness of your communication.

2. Nonverbal communication skills can improve your life in numerous ways, including your relationships, your casual interactions, and your own self talk.

3. When you use body language to influence your own thoughts and feelings, you are using an element of neuro-linguistic programming (NLP).

4. The two areas most associated with the study of body language and the most searched by people seeking information about body language are "liking" and "deception."

5. You can use nonverbal cues to more effectively communicate like and dislike, truth and deception, in a variety of circumstances.

6. You can use nonverbal cues to more effectively respond when you receive like and dislike, truth and deception body language messages from others.

7. Make a point of actively observing body language in the real world so you can continue to learn. You will discover nonverbal behaviors you can adapt for yourself as well as nonverbal behaviors you should avoid.

8. There is a difference between using nonverbal communication skills for influence or for manipulation. In situations where different perspectives may produce different interpretations, integrity and intent are underlying factors to consider.

9. When you choose to use your body language knowledge in positive ways, you can create substantial benefit for yourself as well as the people around you.

Chapter 11 **WORKSHEET**

---

1. Review the Chapter 11 Takeaways and answer the following:
   - Which key point(s) did you find most interesting? Why?
   - Which key point(s) did you find most surprising? Why?

2. Pick four examples from the sections on sending and receiving nonverbal communication in the real world, and describe your own typical body language and nonverbal behaviors in those same circumstances.

    Example 1—Communicating like/dislike

    Example 2—Communicating truth/deception

    Example 3—Receiving like/dislike

    Example 4—Receiving truth/deception

3. Over the next week, observe body language in the world around you. Based on your observations, write down one nonverbal behavior you can adapt for your own use and one nonverbal behavior you will avoid.

12 | Body Language and Other Cultures

B ody language is fascinating enough in respect to American culture, but it becomes truly amazing when examined with respect to other cultures around the world. Some nonverbal behaviors are practically universal and have the same meaning no matter where you go. Others have dramatically different meanings in different countries or regions.

Knowing the difference between what is acceptable and unacceptable in a given culture is not only interesting, it is increasingly critical in our global economy where cultures interact every day and in multiple ways. Whether you are a traveler visiting different countries, a business person with international dealings, or simply someone who interacts with diverse people every day, it is well worth the time and effort to learn as much as you can about body language and other cultures.

Global Similarities and Differences

There are a surprising number of similarities in some body language across cultures, even across cultures separated by vast distances and with no interaction at all. How is this possible? How can one nonverbal behavior mean the same thing in two places located on opposite sides of the planet? The answer, most researchers agree, is based on preprogrammed human characteristics.

In other words, some nonverbal behaviors are innate to human beings and universal across cultures. What are these universal non-verbal behaviors? In short, facial expressions. Research shows that smiling and facial expressions of anger, surprise, fear, happiness, sadness, disgust, and so on, are interpreted the same way in nearly every part of the world. There are some slight differences, such as in Japan where people often have trouble differentiating between expressions of surprise and fear, but these are few in number and minor in significance.

Similarities among facial expressions are so universal, in fact, that researchers studying isolated cultures in New Guinea and West Irian Jaya found people in these tribes recognized and interpreted facial expressions in the same way as others across the rest of the world. This is significant, because the tribes studied had lived for hundreds of years without any contact with the outside world. They were totally isolated and lived completely within the bounds of their own territory and culture, and yet they attached the same meanings to smiling and facial expressions of anger, sadness, and the like.

Despite these similarities, however, there are many more global differences in body language and nonverbal behaviors. The greatest differences and variations are seen in eye contact, touch, gestures, and territorial space, and the regions with the most local differences are Japan, some parts of Asia, and Arab countries. Before we move further along, I need to give you more precise definitions of each category of nonverbal behaviors.

Eye contact—Differences in eye contact include length of eye contact, intensity of eye contact, and even whether or not eye contact is made. Variations may be based on age, social status, hierarchical position, gender, and so on.

Touch—Differences in touch appear in terms of frequency and meaning. This means cultures engage in touching more or less often, and they attach vastly different meanings to different kinds of touch.

Gestures—Differences in gestures occur mostly in terms of insults and vulgarity. They typically involve hands, fingers, and/or the movements of these body parts.

Territorial space—Differences in territorial space occur in terms of personal space, such as how close people stand to each other, and working space, such as offices, living areas, and the like.

Common Cultural Misunderstandings

Now that we have definitions in place we can look at some of the most common cultural misunderstandings in each of these categories.

Eye contact—In Western cultures it is considered normal and acceptable for people of all kinds to make eye contact with each other in most situations, as long as that eye contact is not overly intense. So for instance, when a supervisor speaks with an employee it is appropriate and expected that the two people should make eye contact during the interaction. In Japan, some parts of Asia, and the Middle East, however, employees would be expected to avert their eyes frequently in deference to the supervisor's higher rank in the hierarchy.

Gender differences in eye contact are most pronounced in Arab countries, where interactions between men and women are subject to strict cultural rules. In the strictest countries, women are not allowed to make eye contact with any man who is not a relative, and even that eye contact is limited when in public vs. private environments.

Touch—Regions with the highest frequency of touching include Central America, South America, the Middle East, and southern areas of Europe. In these parts of the world people touch each other regularly during interactions, on the arm, the hand, the back, or even a pat on the knee. In Central America, for instance, when two people are sitting next to or facing each other it is common for them to reach out and touch each other's knees for emphasis during a conversation. This occurs frequently and the meaning is one of friendliness and expressiveness.

In Italy, on the other hand, frequent touching during interactions has a very different meaning. Italians tend to raise their hands and arms during conversation as a way to take the floor and control the interaction. If one person wants to take the floor from another person, he will grasp the arms of the other person and physically hold them down. This allows him to take control of the interaction and become the speaker commanding the most attention.

Gestures—When it comes to insulting and vulgar gestures, there are tremendous differences among cultures. What is acceptable and interpreted positively in one culture can easily be interpreted as a grievous insult in other cultures. I'll focus on three of the most common gestures that cross cultures in vastly different ways—thumbs up, the v-sign, and the ring gesture.

Giving a thumbs up in the United States, Australia, Great Britain, New Zealand, and any other place with a history of British influence means "okay," "good job," or is a signal used to hitch a ride from a passing vehicle. In other countries without that historic British influence, however, a thumbs up hand signal means "up yours," "get stuffed," or some other variation of an insult.

The v-sign (holding two fingers up in a "v" shape) is a sign of victory or acclaim when given with the palm facing outward, but in Great Britain the v-sign has a vastly different meaning when the palm is facing inward toward the person making the gesture. In this form it means "up yours," "piss off," or some similar vulgarity. It is a significant insult and one that is likely to generate a very strong reaction when used during an interaction.

The ring gesture (thumb and index finger forming a circle and the remaining fingers stretched outward) means "okay" in the United States and most other English-speaking countries. In France, however, it means "zero" or "worthless," while in Japan it means "money" and is often interpreted as a request for a bribe of some sort. In the Mediterranean region, Turkey, Greece, and Arab countries the ring gesture is a tremendous insult, implying that someone is a detestable person, or a homosexual, or it may even be interpreted as a threat. The same holds true for Latin American countries as well.

Territorial space—If you travel to Italy or Latin America you will find people stand very close to each other, practically touching in many situations. This is difficult and uncomfortable, though, for people from the United States, Great Britain, and many Asian countries. In Japan especially, territorial space is considered very personal and not to be violated; you will not see people shaking hands, hugging, or otherwise standing in close proximity to each other. There are exceptions to this, though, such as two women or two men walking together and holding hands; to the Japanese this is a sign of friendship.

Territorial space also comes into play during greetings and farewell interactions. For instance, in Scandinavia, France, the Netherlands, Belgium, and most Arab countries, greetings and farewells are usually expressed by kissing on the cheek once, twice, or even three times. In the United States and Great Britain, however, such greetings are awkward and usually avoided as much as possible; a handshake is the preferred greeting or farewell gesture.

The Influence of Culture and History

Culture and history are powerful influences on body language and nonverbal behaviors, sometimes in ways that might surprise you. Here are some examples:

> *Blowing your nose*—In European and Western countries, the modern practice of blowing your nose in a tissue or handkerchief is rooted in preventing the virulent spread of tuberculosis. This

terribly contagious disease spreads through nose secretions and saliva so governments faced with epidemics of tuberculosis launched huge campaigns encouraging people to use tissues and handkerchiefs. The practice went a long way toward helping reduce the spread of the disease.

In Asian countries, especially Japan, just the opposite is true. Their cultural practice is to openly spit or snort mucus and secretions rather than blow them into a tissue. People from these cultures, in fact, are horrified at the thought of blowing your nose into a handkerchief and then putting it into your pocket.

The stiff upper lip—This facial expression is famous and typical of people from Great Britain who use it to avoid displaying emotions. King Henry VIII popularized this facial gesture as an expression of superiority and control in the sixteenth century, and it is still in use today. The effect of the stiff upper lip is perceived as cold, unemotional, and unfriendly by many other cultures, especially those where expressing emotions is expected and considered highly desirable.

The v-sign—I mentioned earlier the different meaning of this gesture, particularly in Great Britain, and the reason for this is rooted in British and European history. Centuries ago when archery was a primary tool in warfare, captured archers often had their two shooting fingers removed as a sign of degradation. It was, for most men, considered a fate much worse than simply being killed.

Because of this, the v-sign was used as a taunt by archers. They would flash the v-sign as a way of saying, "Hey, look, I still have my shooting fingers," and insult the enemy. It became a very powerful insulting gesture in Great Britain that continues unabated today.

American media—Many diverse cultures are now developing body language and nonverbal behaviors that are very American, thanks to the spread of movies and TV from the United States. As our media has spread to the far corners of the world, our common gestures and nonverbal behaviors have spread as well. In many places, younger generations have been exposed to so much American media that they readily pick up and understand American body language, while the older generations still perceive these things in their own traditional ways.

Respect and Accommodation for Others

Even if you don't travel to different countries you are still very likely to encounter situations that require respect and accommodations for the body language of other cultures. In the United States, for example, the mix of cultures is unlike that of nearly any other place in the world. You can walk down the street in some parts of the country and see people from Europe, the Middle East, Asia, South America, and such, all within a short distance. You cannot hope to interact in a positive way with diverse groups of people without being familiar with and understanding their body language and nonverbal behaviors.

Colleges and universities often attract students from around the world. If students are not familiar with each others' nonverbal behaviors, this can lead to misunderstandings and misinterpretations between students as well as between students and professors. A student from Germany or Great Britain is not accustomed to communicating with hand and arm gestures, so when sitting in a class taught by a professor who uses such gestures, these students may feel intimidated.

Another common misunderstanding occurs when interacting with someone from Japan. In that culture, it is considered polite to nod the head and smile when listening to another person as a sign of respect and close attention. In other cultures, however, those same movements are used to indicate agreement with what a person is saying. You can imagine, then, the problems that may arise when a

Westerner interacts with someone from Japan. As the Japanese person nods to show respect, the Westerner perceives agreement.

Any time you travel to another country or will be in contact with people from another culture, you would be wise to familiarize yourself with the body language and nonverbal behaviors typical of that culture. It will help you tremendously when it comes to successful interactions and communication and show your respect for other customs. When you go to another country you are far more likely to be well received if you make the effort ahead of time to learn a bit about what is appropriate and what is not appropriate in that country.

Chapter 12 TAKEAWAYS

1. Body language and nonverbal behaviors have both similarities and differences across different countries and cultures. Awareness and understanding of these differences is critical to successfully interacting with people of varying cultural backgrounds, especially in our increasingly global economy.

2. Smiling and facial expressions such as happiness, anger, sadness, fear, surprise, disgust, and so forth, are innate to human beings and universal across cultures with only occasional slight differences.

3. Cultural differences in body language and nonverbal behaviors typically show up in the areas of eye contact, touch, gestures, and territorial space.

4. Eye contact can vary in length, intensity, and whether or not it occurs at all. Variations may be based on age, social status, hierarchical position, gender, and so on.

5. Touch differs across cultures in terms of frequency and meaning. Different countries have different patterns of frequency in touching—Central America, South America, the Middle

East, and southern Europe show the greatest frequency. The meaning varies as well, such as in Italy where touching someone and holding down his arms is a way of taking center stage during a conversation.

6. Gestures most often have different meanings in terms of insults and vulgarity. The thumbs up, the v-sign, and the ring gesture are the three gestures most commonly interpreted differently across a variety of cultures.

7. Territorial space comes into play during personal interactions and during greeting and farewell interactions. People from Italy and Latin American countries are known for standing very close to each other and having very small territorial spaces, while the custom in the United States, Great Britain, and many Asian countries is just the opposite.

8. Culture and history have a powerful impact on body language and nonverbal behavioral differences. Examples include the history and evolution of behaviors such as blowing your nose, the stiff upper lip facial expression, and the v-sign.

9. Respect and accommodation for others is critical, even if you never leave your own country. Encounters and interactions with people from diverse cultures are common, and if you are not familiar with differences in body language then miscommunications and misunderstandings are likely.

Chapter 12 **WORKSHEET**

---

1. Review the Chapter 12 Takeaways and answer the following:
    - Which key point(s) did you find most interesting? Why?
    - Which key point(s) did you find most surprising? Why?

2. Think about a time when you interacted with someone from another culture. Describe the interaction in terms of:

Eye contact

Touch

Gestures

Territorial space

3. Pick a country that you would like to visit and research its cultural differences. Imagine you are planning a trip to that country, and write down some key talking points on nonverbal behaviors.

- What body language should you avoid?
- What body language should you embrace?

13 | Practical Applications

Here we are, at the final chapter of this book. I am confident you have learned a great deal about body language and nonverbal behaviors so far, and have also gained insight on practical applications for the knowledge you gained.

Practical applications are vital to the study of body language and nonverbal behaviors because they bridge the gap between scientific research and real life. Because of this, I have chosen to close out with an emphasis on practical applications in several situations and circumstances.

Academia

In the academic world, there is a great deal of interaction among and between people with different cultural backgrounds. It is a world where cultures and expectations come together in close quarters and for the purpose of education and study. The pursuit of knowledge, then, is well served when body language and non-verbal behaviors are respected and understood.

Among faculty members, respect for differences is vital for success and focus within and among departments. When professors of different cultural backgrounds work closely together they have an opportunity to learn from each other and influence each other's perspectives.

For instance, I know of a university where the new chair of the communications department was from Japan. He had the credentials and prestige for the position he held, but his cultural background created some initial difficulties for his interactions with department faculty. Faculty meetings prior to his arrival had been casual, open, and sometimes even a bit raucous when the group was enthusiastic about something.

From a Japanese cultural perspective, however, this type of atmosphere was completely foreign. He struggled to lead and direct discussion during the meetings because his nonverbal behavior of nodding when other spoke was interpreted as agreement rather than respect. When he later expressed his own opinions and decisions that ran counter to what was discussed, faculty members often were up in arms over what they perceived as mixed messages. It took concerted effort and understanding for the department to smooth out differences in body language and perceptions.

Another example from academia is when students from different cultures attend a school, regardless of whether it is an elementary school, a middle school, a high school, or college. A student coming to an American school from Great Britain or some Asian countries would find the nonverbal behaviors and body language quite disrespectful to the teachers and uncomfortable in the learning environment. For instance, in Great Britain it is expected in many schools that a student will stand up when addressing the teacher with a question. That is not the custom in most American schools, so it may create a great deal of discomfort and confusion. The same would hold true for the

American student who enrolls in a British school; he would be quite puzzled at the teacher's reaction the first time he posed a question while sitting down.

Even in situations where people in the academic world come from the same cultural background, body language and nonverbal behaviors have a powerful influence. Some professors expect students to show great deference and submission because they view themselves as superior and of higher status. The atmosphere in a classroom like this is vastly different from the atmosphere in a classroom where the professor is more open and casual, encouraging students to join in discussions and voice their opinions.

Elementary school classrooms are another place where you will find many differences in body language expectations. Most teachers who started their careers 15 or 20 years ago will run a classroom with much more structure and strict behavioral expectations; the child who rolls her eyes or has trouble sitting still and straight at his desk is likely to experience difficulty in that class. Students who can adapt their body language and nonverbal behaviors to the teacher's expectations most effectively are likely to experience the greatest comfort and success.

Business

The business world has long been an arena where body language and nonverbal behaviors created all sorts of interesting situations. Two business people negotiating the price or details of a transaction display plenty of body language in action. Each will likely start with very conservative, controlled facial expressions and body position so as not to tip off the other person to what they really think or want. As the negotiations proceed and the two parties come to an agreement, their body language will become more relaxed and comfortable.

Interviewing for a job is another area of the business world where body language and nonverbal behaviors play an important role. The job applicant who walks in the room with confidence, makes good eye contact, and sits with an open body position is likely to be perceived much more positively than the job applicant who walks hesitantly, avoids eye contact, and sits with a closed or nervous body position.

In terms of business across cultures, you can look back centuries to the earliest explorers who visited new lands to trade goods and encountered cultures with vastly different body language norms. Some of the greatest clashes occurred when Western explorers first reached Japan. The Japanese were very formal and structured in their interactions, with a great deal of attention given to proper bowing and submissive behaviors based on rank and status. Western explorers did not understand or appreciate the importance of this and often ridiculed what they perceived as inferior customs and practices.

It is only in recent decades that Western cultures have paid attention to being more culturally sensitive and accommodating of diverse people. Where a business person from the United States might have previously been oblivious to the importance of bowing and nodding in Asian countries, in modern times that business person is likely to become familiar with Asian customs before traveling there. Multinational companies regularly provide training and education to employees who travel to different countries, especially if those employees will be actually living in a different country. Such training is vital for both business and personal success when moving into a different culture.

Diplomacy

Awareness of body language and nonverbal behaviors is an important part of diplomacy, regardless of whether it takes place between different countries or between two people who have a contentious relationship. Knowing the appropriateness of different body language and accurately interpreting the nonverbal behaviors of someone else can mean the difference between success and failure in situations where diplomacy is required.

In the modern international world, great care is taken to accommodate and bridge cultural differences among world leaders when they meet. There are entire teams of protocol and pre-event personnel who go over every detail of an interaction to ensure nothing is missed or misunderstood. This was particularly important during the Cold War years when the United States and Europe regularly squared off against the Soviet Union and Eastern Bloc countries. Even the slightest hint of a misperception could have had dramatic consequences in an environment where both sides had nuclear weapons pointed at each other and standing ready for use.

In terms of negotiations and interactions between individuals, there is a huge potential for misunderstanding when two people have different cultural expectations for body language and nonverbal behaviors. For instance, if a person from Italy and a person from Germany meet to discuss a contentious issue, both need to be aware of each other's common body language. The Italian likely communicates with a great deal of hand and arm movement, which the German will likely find extremely rude and perhaps intimidating. On the flip side of the issue, the German's cultural tendency to show very little body movement and interact in a very structured and disciplined manner is likely to appear cold and inflexible to the Italian. The more contentious the issue, the more these differences potentially affect the outcome and the effectiveness of diplomacy efforts.

Professional mediators spend a great deal of time learning about and practicing their body language and nonverbal behaviors. Their role as objective intermediary charged with reaching a fair agreement means they cannot reveal anything about their thoughts or which side of a disagreement they're on.

Politics

Body language and nonverbal behaviors are integral to successful politics. In the corporate world of office politics, those who are trying to impress the boss are likely to smile at and lean in when the boss is speaking. They will try to grab a seat at the table as close as possible to the boss and will make an extra effort to make conversation and take an interest in the things that the boss deems important.

In terms of governments and the politicians who run for elected office, they literally could not be elected if they were not skilled at using body language and nonverbal behaviors to promote themselves. For instance, picture a candidate walking through a group of people, smiling and shaking hands along the way. Do you think the candidate is really that happy to see those people and intensely interested in meeting them individually? Probably not. The politician is consciously using body language to create the image of a friendly person who truly cares about the needs of each individual person. There is no room for grumpiness, aloofness, or the cold shoulder when it comes to campaigning for elected office.

Presidential campaigns in the United States are particularly interesting to observe in terms of body language. The candidates endure grueling schedules of fund-raisers and campaign stops, yet you will never see one showing signs of being tired or worn down. They make a concerted effort to put on a happy, energetic face; they also have aides and assistants who make sure their hair and makeup looks fresh rather than tired. During primary season the pace of campaigning is frenetic and candidates are actively competing with each other for their party's nomination, so they will take great pains to appear vigorous and enthusiastic.

Once the primary season is over and the major parties have selected their candidates, the pace of campaigning is still frenetic but the body language and nonverbal behaviors change somewhat. The emphasis turns to body language that portrays strength, leadership, and patriotism. Candidates want voters to see them acting "presidential" as a way to help influence how they cast their votes. It all comes to a climax on election night when the winner is announced; he comes before the cameras to make a statement as president-elect and the body language changes tremendously. There is a more regal bearing, confident and measured movements, and a concerted effort to act the way a president is expected to act. The days of easy laughter and relaxed communication are gone, replaced with days of intense scrutiny and interpretation of every movement and expression.

Everyday Life

When it comes to everyday life, it's impossible to list all of the practical applications of body language and nonverbal behaviors. From the time you get up in the morning to the time you go to bed in the evening, your body language communicates clearly and sends powerful messages about you.

For instance, your body language as you stand in front of the mirror getting dressed has a strong influence on your own attitude and perceptions of yourself. Put on a smile and you can help get rid of a negative attitude; stand up straight and look confidently ahead and you can help get rid of nervousness and fear.

Interactions with your family, friends, coworkers, and even total strangers are affected by your body language. Sitting at the breakfast table slumped over communicates to your spouse and children that you are not in the best mood and that they should tread carefully. On the subway, if you sit with an open body position the other passengers are much more likely to make eye contact, smile, and perhaps strike up a conversation with you.

In the office, your body language affects your employees, peers, and even your superiors in the work hierarchy. Successfully coaching an employee requires a specific tone of voice and nonverbal behavior that provides the right amount of encouragement, correction, and guidance. If your body language is not in synch with your coaching intent, then the employee will perceive mixed messages and will not benefit nearly as much from the interaction with you.

Wouldn't it be amazing to have a videotape of yourself throughout the day? You could go back and see yourself the way others see you rather than the way you think they see you. It would quickly become apparent if your body language is sending unintended messages. It would be easy to spot situations where your body language is in conflict with your words and tone of voice. It would truly be an enlightening experience, to say the least.

I encourage you to approach body language and nonverbal behaviors as important aspects of your everyday life. Pay attention to what your body language is saying and consciously choose nonverbal behaviors that are consistent with your words. When you actively choose appropriate body language for whatever it is you want to achieve, you are much more likely to achieve your desired results.

Chapter 13 TAKEAWAYS

1. Practical applications of body language and nonverbal behaviors are vital tools to bridging the scientific study of body language and the realities of the real world.

2. In the academic world, there tend to be many opportunities for interaction with people from diverse cultures. Even in situations where people come from the same cultural background, body language and nonverbal behaviors are important factors in academic interactions.

3. In the business world, body language and nonverbal behaviors are extremely important to nearly every interaction. They

influence negotiations, job interviews, and the overall success of business endeavors.

4. In terms of diplomacy, body language and nonverbal behaviors influence interactions between countries as well as between groups and individuals. The right body language can mean the difference between successful resolution of a conflict and worsening of a situation.

5. In politics, body language and nonverbal behaviors are vital. The office environment is full of body language designed to influence intraoffice politics and gain status or power. Politicians running for elected office are especially attuned to their body language because it is such a powerful communication tool for influencing voting behaviors.

6. In everyday life, body language and nonverbal behaviors are a constant part of everything you do. They influence your own attitude and behavior, the attitude and behavior of people around you, and your effectiveness throughout the day.

Chapter 13 WORKSHEET

---

1. Review the Chapter 13 Takeaways and answer the following:
    - Which key point(s) did you find most interesting? Why?
    - Which key point(s) did you find most surprising? Why?

2. Think about your experience in academics or the business world, and describe a situation where body language or nonverbal behavior had an impact.
    - What were the positive impacts?
    - What were the negative impacts?
    - What did you learn from your experience?

3. Pick a politician at any level of government—city, county, state, or national—and watch what he does in terms of body language and nonverbal behaviors.

- What body language do you observe most often?
- What effect does that body language have?
- If it were campaign season, how would you expect the body language to change when the election is over?
- If it were not campaign season, how would you expect the body language to change when it comes times to run for re-election?

Bibliography

Brenner, Robert C. *Body Language in Business*. San Diego: Brenner Information Group, 2004.

Briton, NJ and Hall JA. "Beliefs about Male and Female Nonverbal Communication." *Sex Roles* 32 (1995): 79–90.

Givens, David. *Love Signals*. New York: St. Martins Press, 2005.

Hall, Edward. *The Silent Language*. Garden City, NY: Anchor Books, 1959.

Hitsch, Gunter J., Ali, Hortaçsu, and Dan Ariely. "What Makes You Click?—Mate Preferences and Matching Outcomes in Online Dating." MIT Sloan School of Management Working Paper (February 2006).

Hogan, Kevin. *Covert Persuasion*. Hoboken: Wiley & Sons, 2006.

Hogan, Kevin. *Irresistible Attraction: Secrets of Personal Magnetism*. Minneapolis: Network 3000 Publishing, 2000.

Hogan, Kevin. *The Psychology of Persuasion: How to Persuade Anyone to Your Way of Thinking*. Gretna, LA: Pelican Publishing, 1996.

Knapp, Mark L., and Judith A. Hall. *Nonverbal Communication in Human Interaction*. Texas: Thomson Learning, Inc., 2002.

Manusov, Valerie, Patterson, Miles. *Sage Handbook of Nonverbal Communication*. Thousand Oaks, CA. Sage Publications, 2006.

Mehrabian, Albert. "Orientation Behaviors and Nonverbal Communication." *Journal of Communication* 17: 324–332.

Morris, Desmond. *The Meaning of Human Gestures*. New York: Crown, 1994.

Bibliography

Pease, Alan. *Body Language: How to Read Others' Thoughts by Their Gestures.* London: Orion Publishing, 2004.

Pease, Alan and Barbara. *The Definitive Book of Body Language.* London: Orion Publishing, 2006.

The Body Language Home Study Course

Learning the basics of body language, and even learning some powerful advanced skills, can be accomplished from reading a book.

That said, there is a lot that has to do with micro-expressions of the human face that I can't teach you in a book. It's also impossible to communicate the actual "reading" of vocal intonation, pitch, and matching or not matching those cues with all kinds of nonverbal cues.

What you learned in this book can help you earn thousands of dollars more annually. It will change your life.

What you learn in the Body Language Home Study Course will put you on the level of the nonverbal communication masters.

Use **YOURCOURSE** as your discount code when you check out and you will save $100 off the already discounted price in the store at www.kevinhogan.com. No one else in the world has this coupon code. It's my way of saying thank you for taking a chance on reading *The Secret Language of Business*.

The link for you to use to read all about what's in this truly groundbreaking and comprehensive multimedia and interactive home study course is

www.kevinhogan.com/bodylanguage.htm

Need a Speaker for Your Company or Convention's Next Meeting?

There is a special web site that will meet your needs: www. kevinhogan.net.

I've put together the most entertaining, instructive, humorous, educational way to learn about body language and nonverbal communication in the world. About two-thirds of the groups bring me in for a half day. The other one-third bring me in for the day.

We get a lot done, have a lot of fun, and go home at the end of the day with a "wow."

You can get hold of us through the web site, and we'll be at your service immediately.

Index